I CAN READ THAT!

I CAN READ THAT!

A Traveler's Introduction to Chinese Characters

---

by JULIE MAZEL SUSSMAN

CHINA BOOKS
& Periodicals, Inc.
San Francisco

一九九四年

Book design by Ella Mazel
Cover design by Linda Revel
Handwritten Chinese characters by 小王 (J. J. King)

Typeset Chinese characters are from the TwinBridge
Chinese System by PC Express, Inc.

5 7 9 10 8 6 4

Library of Congress Catalog Card Number: 94-094622
ISBN 0-8351-2533-5

Printed in Canada

 China Books & Periodicals, Inc.
2929 Twenty-Fourth Street
San Francisco, CA 94110

ABOUT THE AUTHOR

Julie Sussman studied French, Russian, and German in school, and Chinese, Japanese, Norwegian, Swedish, Dutch, Hebrew, and Serbo-Croatian for trips.

An M.I.T. graduate, in real life she has mostly written software, but recently she has turned to writing and editing books, mainly in computer science.

Contents

Facts about Chinese

Acknowledgments

This book is dedicated to Gerald Jay Sussman, who inspired me to write it. Jerry learned a few characters while we were in China, and had so much fun recognizing "his" characters that he convinced me I should learn some before my second trip. My search for a book that would teach me simple, common characters ended in failure, but I managed to pick out some characters I thought were appropriate and learn them. Jerry was right: It *was* fun to recognize characters. So we decided someone should write the book I had tried to buy.

The photographs in this book were taken by me, Gerald Jay Sussman, Joyce Friedman, and my parents, Bernard and Ella Mazel. The souvenirs (tickets, etc.) in the figures were brought back from China by me, Joyce Friedman, Brian LaMacchia, and Ella Mazel. Special thanks to Ella Mazel for lugging home the Coca-Cola can. And thanks to all you friends and relatives for giving us this opportunity to answer your perennial question, "Why do you keep that junk?" We always knew it was good for something, even if we didn't know what.

Feng Zhao answered many questions about characters and their usage. Many other people helped by letting me try ideas or book drafts on them. I'm grateful for all their suggestions. Bernie Mazel's reactions were the most influential: He challenged me to make this introduction to characters intriguing even to people who didn't think they wanted to learn about Chinese characters.

I CAN READ THAT!

1   ⸺

Is this book for you?

YES, if you are going to China, even for just a few days.

YES, if you are curious about Chinese characters.

YES, whether or not you know, or plan to learn, any spoken Chinese.

Chinese is written using thousands of characters, many of which are quite complicated. To learn to read Chinese, you would have to learn the Chinese language and at least a couple of thousand characters.

But there are also many simple Chinese characters, whose meaning you can learn with very little effort and without learning the spoken language.

If you visit China, you will be surrounded by Chinese characters. You'll find that it is great fun (and sometimes even useful) to be able to recognize some of them. And you will find that "your" characters will jump out at you.

Even if you are not going to China itself, you may still find this book useful, because many of the characters can be seen in other Chinese-speaking communities, such as Hong Kong and Taiwan. The Japanese writing system also includes Chinese characters, even though Japanese and Chinese are completely unrelated languages. (Similarly, English, Finnish, and Swahili all use the Latin alphabet.)

7 characters in 7 minutes

Here are three simple characters. I'll bet you can remember them even if you look at them only once.

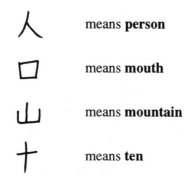

一   means **one**

二   means **two**

三   means **three**

Here are some more simple characters. To remember these, you might think of *person* as a simple stick figure emphasizing the person's two legs, of *mouth* as an open mouth, of *mountain* as having three peaks, and of *ten* as a Roman numeral *X* turned on its side or as a lowercase *t* (for *ten*).

人   means **person**

口   means **mouth**

山   means **mountain**

十   means **ten**

To see whether you remember these characters, try matching up the characters with their meanings in this mixed-up list:

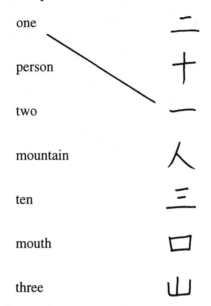

one

person

two

mountain

ten

mouth

three

You already know enough to learn to read some longer words:

三十二　　　means **thirty-two**
　　　　　　(three tens plus two)

山口　　　　means **mountain pass**

人人　　　　means **everybody**

If that was not incredibly mysterious and difficult, read on.

About this book

This book teaches 71 Chinese characters, which I chose because they are relatively simple and are very commonly seen in China. (Outside China, some characters will be different — see "Simplified characters" on page 6 — and some will be less common than they are in China.)

My purpose is to teach you to recognize the characters. But I also show you how to write them, because many people find that writing the characters makes it easier to remember them.

You should start by reading Chapter 2. Then go on to Chapters 3 through 20 to learn <u>new characters</u>, Chapter 21 to see <u>longer words and phrases</u> made out of these characters, and Chapters 22 and 23 to <u>test your knowledge</u>.

You don't have to study the chapters in order or learn all the characters in each chapter. Concentrate on those that look easy or useful to you, and feel free to skip the others. If you see a character that you didn't study or don't remember, you can look it up in the **English Word Index**, the **Pinyin Index**, or the **Quick Reference**.

ABOUT CHINESE

(Sample box). Scattered through this book are a number of "About Chinese" boxes like this one. These contain supplementary information that I hope will add to your understanding and enjoyment, but which is not part of the basic explanations.

2

How to understand this book

In the following chapters, characters are presented like this when they are first taught:

kǒu p.120	⌷	**mouth, opening**
chǎng (s) p.115	厂	**factory**

This layout makes it easy for you to cover up part of the page in order to quiz yourself.

<u>Left</u>	<u>Middle</u>	<u>Right</u>
The Chinese **pronunciation** (a syllable), in Pinyin [see p.7]	The **character**	The **meaning** (or main meaning), in English [see p.6]
(s) if the character is **"simplified"** [see p.6]		
The number of the page in Chapter 24 that shows **how to write** the character [see p.8]		

Meaning

As you saw in Chapter 1, a Chinese word is written as one or more characters, each of which has a meaning. When a character has many senses (just as an English word may have), I will give the most basic, common ones. You may have noticed above that I added a more general meaning, *opening*, for the *mouth* character I introduced in Chapter 1. There are other meanings we won't be concerned with, just as we are not often concerned with many of the meanings of *mouth* in English.

Simplified characters

In the 1950's, the government of the People's Republic of China started to replace certain of the more complicated *traditional characters* with *simplified characters*. I emphasize simplified characters in this book, because they are more often seen in China today than their traditional equivalents. The traditional forms of simplified characters are shown on page 132. Of course, many traditional characters were already very simple, so most of the characters in this book have only one version.

ABOUT CHINESE

Simplified characters outside China. Some of the simplified characters were abbreviations that were already in informal use, while others were devised by the Chinese government. Some of the simplifications that were in general use may be seen in Taiwan, Hong Kong, or other "overseas Chinese" communities, and even in Japan. The government-devised simplifications are seen only in China.

Pronunciation and the Pinyin phonetic alphabet

Pinyin is the official representation of Chinese pronunciation in the Latin alphabet. My purpose in using it is not to teach you to pronounce Chinese — you'll need a tape or teacher for that. But the Pinyin is useful if you already know some spoken Chinese. And it is useful for looking up the characters in the "Pinyin Index" at the end of this book or in a Chinese-English dictionary that is arranged alphabetically by Pinyin spelling. If you want to know a little about Pinyin notation and Chinese pronunciation, look at the sample pronunciations on page 26 and at the overview starting on page 129.

You'll find yourself learning Pinyin spellings of characters whenever you discover that characters you recognize make up a familiar place name. If you visit Beijing, for example, it's fun to know that 北京, which you'll recognize as *north capital*, is spelled *Beijing*. In Sichuan province you'll be delighted to learn that 四川, which you'll know as *four rivers*, is spelled *Sichuan*. I'll point out characters that are common in names as we go along. And Chapter 20 concentrates on place names.

ABOUT CHINESE

Dialects and pronunciations. Pinyin spellings represent the standard pronunciation of the official national language of China, which the Chinese call *pŭtōnghuà* (common speech) and which we call Mandarin Chinese. Of course, there are regional differences in pronunciation in China. And the pronunciation of Cantonese Chinese is very different from that of Mandarin Chinese, though the same characters are used.

ABOUT CHINESE

Use of the Pinyin phonetic alphabet. Attempts have been made over the years to supplement or replace China's character-based writing with an alphabetic (phonetic) system that spells out the sounds. The current system, called Pinyin, represents Chinese pronunciation in the Latin alphabet. China's adoption of Pinyin is the reason that *Peking* became *Beijing* and *Mao Tse-tung* became *Mao Zedong*.

Pinyin is used in this book to indicate pronunciations of Chinese characters and words. You will also see Pinyin writing in China (for example, on money — see the top figure on page 65). But how widely Pinyin will be used in China, and for what, remains to be seen.

How to write characters

You may wish to learn to write characters (for example, to date letters to your Chinese friends), or you may wish to write or trace characters as an aid to remembering what they look like.

If you write a character at all, you should draw the strokes in the right order and direction, as shown in Chapter 24. If you write a character any old way, slight variations in your writing could produce an illegible character or a different character altogether.

Knowing how a character is written will also help you see differences between similar-looking characters, and may help you guess whether something that looks a little different from one of "your" characters is really the same one. For example, if you know that *mouth* 口 is written with three strokes, as shown here

you can understand that it could come out with gaps, but not in the upper right corner.

3 三

People

One of the most common characters you'll see is

rén
p.118
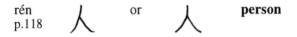
or   **person**

The first form is the normal handwritten form; the second is common in printed matter. (This variation is analogous to the difference between printed and handwritten forms of lowercase *a* in English.) Either version is easy to remember as a stick figure of two legs.

人 is frequently seen with the character

mín
p.128

the people, **folk**

as follows:
the people

This compound word means *the people*, as in *The People's Republic of China*. You'll see 人民 everywhere — in names of institutions, streets, and hotels; on money and stamps; and so on.* You'll also see its Pinyin spelling *renmin* in names.

Don't be disturbed that 民 and 人民 are both defined as meaning *the people*. The two-character (two-syllable) version is an independent word; the single character is used only as part of longer words.

---

* See Figures 1 (page 10), 12 (page 30), 36 (page 62), 38 (page 64), and 48 (page 76).

Although 民 appears in many other compound words, 人民 is by far the most common context, so even if you recognize it only in this two-character word, you'll recognize it a lot. (Some other common uses of 民 are for: nationalities, such as China's ethnic minorities; *folk*, as in *folk music*.)

Notice that 民 means *the people* (as in "government of the people, by the people, for the people"); it is not the ordinary plural *people* of *person* (as in "There were 17 people in my tour group."). Chinese nouns don't have separate singular and plural forms, so the plural of 人 is simply 人.

ABOUT CHINESE

Pluralization and conjugation. Chinese nouns don't have singular and plural forms. So you don't have to learn different forms such as *person/people* or even *mouth/mouths*; all nouns behave like *deer* in English. Other parts of the sentence, rather than a change in the noun, indicate whether the noun is singular or plural. Similarly, verbs aren't conjugated, so you don't have to learn different forms such as *go/goes/went* or even *learn/learns/learned*.

FIGURE 1: Street name in a postcard caption

宽敞笔直的人民南路

Broad and straight People's South Road

The street name (*People's South Road*) is the last four characters of the caption. *South* 南 is explained in Chapter 15. The end of a street name may be this word for *road* or one of many other words, corresponding to *avenue*, *street*, and so on in English.

Gender

The next two characters appear on rest rooms. You will usually use rest rooms meant for tourists, which are labeled in English or with pictures. But for those occasions where you need to use a public facility, these come in handy.

nǚ
p.128

女

female

nán
p.127

男

male

男 is the most complicated character we've seen so far, and one of the most complicated in this book. It's much easier to remember if you know that it is made by combining two other characters: A *male* 男 uses *strength* 力 working in the *field* 田. The character 田 is a picture of a field divided into plots.

lì
p.125

力

strength, power, ability

tián
p.120

田

field, farmland

Peace

A *woman* 女 under a roof represents *peace*:

ān
p.128

安

peace

安 is a very popular word for use in place names, such as Chang'*an* (long/lasting peace) Avenue in Beijing, Tian'*an*men (heavenly peace gate) Square in Beijing, and the city of Xi'*an* (western peace).

Recognizing characters without remembering them in detail

You will often be able to recognize a character in context even though you don't remember it in detail and wouldn't feel sure of it if you saw it alone.

For example, you may think that *the people* 民 is too hard to remember in detail. But all you really have to remember is that it often follows *person* 人, which is easy, and that it resembles a capital R.

And if you care about 男 and 女 only in order to distinguish one restroom entrance from the other, all you need is some way to remember which is which. Or you could learn just one of them.

Compound words

Here are some longer words made out of characters from this chapter. Notice how in the first three compound words the first word modifies the second word, just as it does in English: *person power*, *male person*, *female person*.

人 力	**manpower**
男 人	**man**
女 人	**woman**
男 女	**men and women**
人 人	**everybody**

FIGURE **2**: Restroom signs

Top left: At the Great Wall. The character after *male* and *female* means *toilet*.

Top right: At the site of a tomb in the countryside.

Bottom: Along the Burma Road. This public facility has a two-syllable word for *toilet* and an arrow pointing to the *female* entrance.

4   囚

Size

You might think of *big* 大 as a *person* 人 with outstretched arms. *Medium* 中, which also means *middle* (see page 38), is represented by a vertical line through the middle of a box. You'll have to think up your own way of remembering *small* 小.

dà p.118	大	**big**
zhōng p.121	中	**medium, middle, center**
xiǎo p.122	小	**small**

The general concept of size is represented by a two-syllable combination of *big* and *small*:

大 小   **size**

Big-big is also a word:

大 大   **greatly**

One place you will see these characters is on schools,

xué	(s)	学	**learn, study, school**
p.117			

which come in three sizes (or at least the students come in three sizes):

小 学	**elementary (primary, grammar) school**
中 学	**middle school**
大 学	**university, college**

中学 (which is divided into junior middle school and senior middle school) covers the years between 小学 and 大学. It is equivalent to junior high school (or middle school) plus high school in the United States.

Another important word that contains a size character is *caution* 小心, explained on page 50.

FIGURE 3: "Tianjin University"

The first two characters say *Tianjin*. (天 is explained on page 27.)

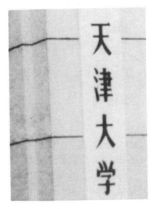

---

5   五

Goods and services

Here are two very simple characters:

gōng
p.115
　　　　　工　　　　　**work**, **worker**

chǎng   (s)
p.115
　　　　　厂　　　　　**factory**

This *factory* character is normally preceded either by *work*, to form the two-syllable word for just plain *factory*

工厂　　　　　**factory**

or by characters that tell what kind of factory it is (see the top figures on pages 18 and 47).

Here is what the 工厂 produces. I think of it as a pile of cartons.

pǐn
p.120
　　　　　品　　　　　**goods**, **products**,
　　　　　　　　　　　　　　　articles

The 品 are sold in a

diàn
p.124
　　　　　店　　　　　**store**, **shop**

店 is generally preceded by characters that indicate the kind of store (see Figure 4).

You will also see 店 at the end of many hotel and restaurant names, since it appears at the end of a word that means both *hotel* and *restaurant* (see Figures 5 and 6).

FIGURE 4: "Yanjing bookstore"

The first two characters say *Yanjing* (京 is explained on page 78) and the next is *book*; the last two characters together mean *bookstore*.

FIGURE 5: "Beijing Hotel" buffet ticket

The first two characters on top say *Beijing* (page 78); the last two mean *hotel*. The bottom line says *meal coupon*.

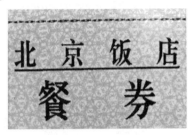

FIGURE 6: "Beijing Restaurant" in Norway

The Chinese name *Beijing Restaurant* of this restaurant in Trondheim, Norway, is the same as the name of the *Beijing Hotel* in China (Figure 5). It looks different because the character before 店 here is the traditional version of the simplified character used in Figure 5.

FIGURE 7: "Tianjin Carpets Factory No.3"

Factories are often numbered. Notice that the number comes right before the word 厂. Literally, the name is *Tianjin municipality* (see page 27 for 天 and page 68 for 市) *carpet* (next two characters) *three factory*.

天津市
地毯三厂

FIGURE 8: "Kodak products" are available here

柯达产品

The first two characters on this sign in Xi'an were chosen to sound somewhat like *Kodak* (they say *Kē dá*); the last two form the two-syllable version of *product*.

ABOUT CHINESE

Writing foreign words and names. When a foreign word or name is used in China, it is transliterated into Chinese by using characters that approximate the way it sounds. Since there are generally many characters whose pronunciation is reasonably close, and characters have meanings as well as sounds, characters are sometimes chosen to create an appropriate meaning for the foreign name (e.g., *Coca-Cola* in Chapter 19). The Chinese transliteration of *Kodak* (above), however, doesn't mean anything.

---

6 六

Openings and closings

From the word for *mouth* 口, which looks like an open mouth, we get the *entrance* and *exit* signs that appear on doorways. (The mouth is squarish because there are no circular shapes in Chinese characters.) Another place you'll frequently see 口 is on Coca-Cola cans (page 73).

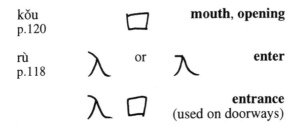

kǒu
p.120
mouth, opening

rù
p.118
or
enter

entrance
(used on doorways)

入 口 also means, quite literally, *enter the mouth*.

The first form of *enter* is the normal handwritten form; the second is common in printed matter. (This variation is analogous to the different forms of lowercase *a* in English.)

Don't confuse *enter* with *person* (page 9). In the usual handwritten forms, they are mirror images.

person: 人   enter: 入

In their other forms *person* is symmetrical, and the part of *enter* that sticks out at the top is folded over to the left.

person: 人   enter: 入

The *exit* character 出 has a wide range of uses in words for which there is an English expression containing the word *out*. For example, it is the first character of *taxi* (as part of "rent out" — see Figure 25 on page 48) and of *publish* (in the sense of "issue" or "put out" — see Figure 76 on page 111).

| chū
p.119 | 出 | **exit, produce** |

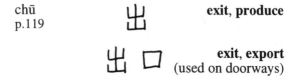

| | 出 口 | **exit, export**
(used on doorways) |

The next word appears in place names such as Tian'an*men* (heavenly peace gate — see page 76) and Qian*men* (front gate) in Beijing.

| mén (s)
p.128 | 门 | **door, gate** |

You probably won't come across *doorway*, but it's a compound word whose parts are familiar:

| | 门 口 | **doorway** |

Here's what you can do to a 门, or to a light or switch. You might see 开 and 关 labeling switches or indicating what days or hours a place is open.

| kāi (s)
p.119 | 开 | **open, turn on** |

| guān (s)
p.119 | 关 | **close, turn off** |

In fact, a *switch* is called a

| 开 关 | **switch** |

Here's what a store does:

开 门   **open** [the doors]

关 门   **close** [the doors]

FIGURE 9: "Exit" and "enter" signs

The exit sign below was in Tokyo's Narita airport. The other two signs were in China. You'll see the same entrance and exit signs wherever Chinese characters are used.

FIGURE 10: On/off switch

Here's a sketch of the 开关 (switch) on the bottom of the battery-operated panda I bought in China.

7 七

Numbers

Words versus numerals

You don't need to know the characters for numbers in order to use money, read prices, tell time, or find your hotel room. Arabic numerals are used for these purposes, as you are accustomed to. But just as we sometimes write *ninety* instead of *90*, so do the Chinese. It is quite easy to learn to recognize the words for numbers from 1 to 99, and to learn to read dates (Chapters 8 and 9). You will see small numbers on many kinds of signs, and you will see dates written with characters on plaques at tourist attractions.

1-10

yī p.114	一	**one**
èr p.114	二	**two**
sān p.114	三	**three**
sì p.121	四 or 四	**four**
wǔ p.117	五	**five**
liù p.116	六	**six**

qī p.113	七	**seven**
bā p.114	八 or 八	**eight**
jiǔ p.125	九	**nine**
shí p.113	十	**ten**

The first form of *four* shown above is the standard form, but the other is seen occasionally.

The first form of *eight* is the normal handwritten form; the second is common in printed matter.

11-99

Numbers from eleven to ninety-nine are just combinations of the above characters. You simply give the number of tens followed by the number of ones, as in English. But the Chinese way of doing this is simpler than the English way. In English, we must learn special words for the numbers of tens — thirty, ninety, etc. — while in Chinese we just say three-ten(s), nine-ten(s), etc. (But note that for numbers from 11 to 19 you just say ten, not one-ten.)

Here are some sample numbers:

十 四	**fourteen** (ten four)
四 十	**forty** (four tens)
七 十 八	**seventy-eight** (seven tens eight)

You might want to practice writing the numbers from 1 to 99. Or cut out the characters facing page 36 and arrange them to make these numbers.

How to learn the numbers

1-3: If only everything were as easy as 一 二 三 !

4-10: Notice that the even numbers 4 四, 6 六, 8 八, and 10 十 are symmetrical (well, almost symmetrical), while the odd numbers 5 五, 7 七, and 9 九 are asymmetrical. Also, notice the similar pair of lines in the even numbers 4, 6, and 8, which I have darkened in the following: 四 六 八

Think of this pair as standing for 2: Each number that has this pair of lines is even (divisible by 2). (If you know some French, you might recall that *pair* is French for *even*.)

To remember 10 十, you may want to think of a Roman numeral *X* turned on end.

Some people see a 5 embedded in 五 五

You'll find 7 七 easy to remember if you're familiar with the European-style 7, which looks like the Chinese character if you turn the page upside-down.

1-12: Practice telling time, using the clock on the next page.

1-31: Make some familiar years and dates (family birthdays, historical events, and so on), as explained in Chapters 8 and 9. If you look at dates in the 1900's, for example, you will soon know the number 9 九 very well, and you will not confuse it with *strength* 力 (page 11). You may either write the dates, or cut out the characters facing page 36.

FIGURE 11: A clock for number practice

Real clocks use numerals, not characters. But this clock may help you learn the characters for the numbers. You can make hands for the clock out of toothpicks or paper.

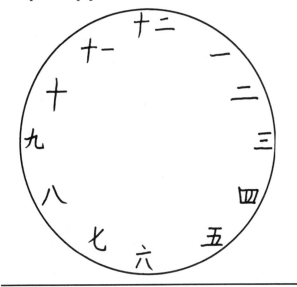

Confusing things: *Eight* may seem similar to *person* (page 9) or *enter* (page 19).

eight: 八　person: 人　enter: 入

eight: 八　person: 人　enter: 入

You can tell the symmetrical *eight* and *person* apart by noticing that the two "legs" of *eight* don't touch, while the "legs" of *person* do. You can tell the *eight* and *enter* with folded-over lines apart by noticing that the right stroke sticks out over the left stroke in *enter* but not in *eight*. But you'll generally know from the context whether to expect a number, so remembering how to tell *eight* from the other possibilities isn't very important for recognition.

Fun with numbers

In the hotel, you normally leave your key with a floor attendant when you go out and request it by room number when you come in. The attendant will understand English, but it is fun to try to say the room number in Chinese and see if you get the right key. You should just say a sequence of digits. That is, just say *èr sān sì* (*two three four*) rather than trying to say *two hundred thirty-four* or *two thirty-four*. If your number contains a 0, say *líng*.* (The character for *zero* wasn't shown above because it is very complicated. You won't see it on your room or key, however, since room numbers are written with numerals, not characters.)

In one hotel where I did this, the attendant got a real kick out of it. He laughed the first few times, and after that he remembered me and gave me the right key (still with a big grin) before I could ask.

---

* If you don't know how to read Pinyin, pronounce the numbers like the uppercase parts of these English words:

líng	0	LING as in **LING**uist
yī	1	EA as in **EA**sy
èr	2	**ARE**
sān	3	SAN as in **SAN**ity or SON as in **SON**ic
sì	4	SI as in **SI**r
wǔ	5	OO as in **OO**dles
liù	6	LYOWE as in real**LY OWE**
		(pronouncing <u>LYOWE</u> as a single syllable)
qī	7	CHEE as in **CHEE**tah
bā	8	BA as in **BA**rk
jiǔ	9	**JOE**
shí	10	SHI as in **SHI**rt

8 八

The heavens

These heavenly characters are used in dates, as we will see in Chapter 9, and in place names.

rì p.120	日	**sun, day of the month**
yuè p.126	月	**moon, month**
tiān p.118	天	**sky, heaven, day**

天 is the *tian* of *Tianjin* (see figures on pages 15 and 18) and *Tian'anmen* (page 76).

Bright things

The *sun* 日 and the *moon* 月 combined into a single character give *bright*.

míng p.127	明	**bright, clear**

明 is the *ming* of *Ming dynasty* fame (1368-1644). 明 is also the *ming* of *Kunming* (see billboard on page 47).

You probably won't see this word, but isn't it nice to know that *tomorrow* is a *bright day*?

明 天   **tomorrow**

Months

If you know the numbers from 1 to 12 (Chapter 7), you know the names of the months, since these are just called *one-month*, ..., *twelve-month*.

一月	**January**
二月	**February**
三月	**March**
四月	**April**
五月	**May**
六月	**June**
七月	**July**
八月	**August**
九月	**September**
十月	**October**
十一月	**November**
十二月	**December**

One character or two?

Notice that the single character 明 (made out of the characters for *sun* and *moon*) is not the same as the sequence of characters 日 月 (a compound word, literally *sun-moon* or *day-month*).

日 月 **life, livelihood**

It's easy to distinguish a compound character from a sequence of characters, because characters in a sequence are evenly spaced and each occupies the same amount of space. (Look at the figure on the next page, for example. You'll have no trouble seeing that there are nine characters on the postcard.)

ABOUT CHINESE

Characters made out of other characters. There are a few examples in this book of characters that are made out of a combination of other characters.

男 *male* = 田 *field* + 力 *strength* (page 11)

明 *bright* = 日 *sun* + 月 *moon* (page 27)

林 *forest* = 木 *tree* + 木 *tree* (page 42)

品 *products* = 3 *mouths* 口 (page 16)

You may come across other characters made out of characters you recognize. Please don't waste too much time trying to guess their meaning. As you see from 品, the meaning of a character is not necessarily related to the meaning of its parts.

FIGURE **12**: "Postcard"

中国人民邮政明信片

Postcard

People's Republic of China

明 is also the first syllable of *postcard*. The first six characters say *China People['s] Postal Service*. The last three characters say *postcard*.

Some doubled words

Two of the characters from this chapter combine with themselves to form two-syllable adverbs:

天天　　**every day, daily**

明明　　**clearly, obviously**

9　九

Dates

Dates are written with the year first, then the month, and finally the day.* They may be written with numerals (1965.12.30**) or spelled out:

one nine six five YEAR twelve MONTH thirty DAY

一　九　六　五　年　　十　二　月　　　三　十　日

Notice that the year is written as a sequence of digits (*one nine six five*), not as a single big number (*one thousand nine hundred sixty-five*), while the month and day are each written as a single number, not as a sequence of digits (e.g. *twelve*, not *one two*). The months were shown in Chapter 8.

Dates may also be written as a combination of numerals and words:

> 1965 YEAR 12 MONTH 30 DAY
>
> 1965 年　　12 月　　　30 日

You will have no trouble recognizing the word

nián　　　　　　年　　　　　　**year**
p.119

in dates, because you will recognize all the numbers near it, as well as the words *month* 月 and *day of month* 日 from Chapter 8.

---

* Addresses and people's names are also written with the largest unit first — see box on page 68.
** Dates may also be written as in Europe — 30/12/65 — but this is less common.

Zero in a year is generally written with a big round O instead of with the Chinese character for *zero*, which we haven't learned. (See Figure 14.) Because the character for *zero* is complicated, the round O is used instead in western-style number sequences (phone numbers and years).

FIGURE 13: Part of a piece of currency

In what year was this bill issued? (See page 135 for answer.)

FIGURE 14: Paragraph from a pamphlet

You should be able to read four years in this paragraph. (See page 135 for answer.)

一九五〇年考入中央戏剧学院附属舞蹈团。一九五一年在柏林世界青年联欢节表演《西藏舞》（集体舞）获金质奖。一九五五年在华沙青年联欢节表演双人舞《飞天》再次获奖。一九八〇年第一届全国舞蹈比赛的观摩演出中，获优秀表演奖。

ABOUT CHINESE

Punctuation. Don't be surprised to see familiar-looking punctuation in Chinese text (as in Figure 14). This has been adopted from the West.

ABOUT CHINESE

Word separation (or the lack thereof). Notice (e.g., in Figure 14) that there is no space between words in written Chinese. Most people accustomed to modern alphabetic writing systems* find this strange. We are so used to separating written words that we don't stop to notice that we don't separate most spoken words.

Indeed, the lack of word separation makes reading much harder for a beginning reader or someone who doesn't know the language well. But the same is true of understanding spoken language. Without spaces it is harder to pick out the parts you understand.** Butasafluentspeakerof Englishyoucanreadthissimplesentence, just as you can understand it if you hear it.

Actually, that example of run-on English is an exaggeration of the situation in Chinese, because each Chinese character represents a whole syllable. So a fair er ex am ple would be an En glish sen tence with e ven ly spaced syl la bles. Again, your ability to group the syllables (to know that *am* is part of *example*, not a word itself) depends on your knowledge of English.

That still exaggerates the situation, because a Chinese character doesn't "spell" the sound of the syllable it represents. Sound-alike syllables with different meanings are written with different characters (like *I* and *eye* in English). So in our English example, the *am* of *example* would be written differently from the word *am*.

---

* Thai is written without word spacing, as was biblical Hebrew.
** And the fact that speech is "continuous" is one reason why progress in making computers understand normal speech — as opposed to isolated words — has been slow.

FIGURE 15: Pages from desk calendars

If you had these calendars, you wouldn't have to remember that "Thirty days hath September …" because you could see that April is a *small* 小 month (30 or fewer days) and May is a *big* 大 one (31 days). You could also learn that the third lunar month (see "The Chinese lunar calendar" on page 35) that year was 大 (30 days — a 小 lunar month has only 29 days).

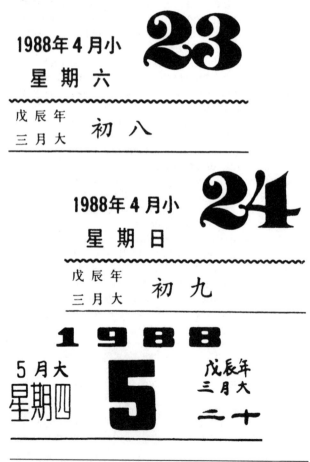

1988年4月小
星 期 六

戊 辰 年
三 月 大　　初 八

1988年4月小
星 期 日

戊 辰 年
三 月 大　　初 九

1988

5月大　　5　　戊辰年
星期四　　　　　三月大
　　　　　　　　二 十

Days of the week

The days of the week (except for *Sunday*) consist of the two-character word for *week* followed by the character for a number from 1 (for Monday) to 6 (for Saturday). *Sunday* has *day* (usually 日, but possibly 天) instead of a number. In the calendar pages in Figure 15, the day of the week is right under the year and month. What days of the week are shown? (See page 135 for answer.)

The word for *week* is quite difficult, so we won't study it in detail. But if you see two complicated characters (the first of which contains *day/sun* 日 on top and the second of which contains *month/moon* 月 as its right half) followed by a single number from 1 to 6 or by either of the characters for *day*, it is probably a day. What day of the week was April 25, 1988 (see Figure 16)? (Answer on page 136.)

FIGURE 16: Newspaper date

PEOPLE'S DAILY

OVERSEAS EDITION

1988 年 4 月 25 日　星 期 一

戊辰 年 三 月初十　第 1013 號

The Chinese lunar calendar

In Figures 15 and 16 you've probably noticed some additional numbers and occurrences of the words *year* 年 and *month* 月 that don't look like the dates you have learned to recognize. These are dates in the lunar calendar.

The Chinese still use their traditional lunar calendar in addition to the Gregorian calendar (which is the one we use). You don't have to know about the lunar calendar when you visit China, because the Gregorian calendar was officially adopted there after the 1911 revolution. But you will see lunar dates along with Gregorian dates on calendars and newspapers, and many traditional holidays are determined by the lunar calendar. In May 1988, for example, I attended the "Third Month Fair" in Dali (in western Yunnan province).

ABOUT CHINESE

Lunar dates. In a lunar date:

The year has a two-character name rather than a number (see the two characters before *year* 年 in Figures 15 and 16). There are sixty names, after which the cycle starts over. The sixty-year cycle is divided into five twelve-year cycles, in which each year is associated with an animal.

The months are named *one-month*, *two-month*, ... Thus *four-month* 四 月 out of context could be either *April* or the fourth lunar month.

The dates are numbered from 1 to 30. (A lunar month has 29 or 30 days.) Lunar dates are always written with characters, not numerals. Dates from 1 to 10 are preceded by a character meaning *first* (see the figures). This is because the month used to be divided into three groups of days each numbered 1-10, so it was necessary to say which group of 10 days was intended. The current 1-10 used to be the "first" 1-10 and is still labeled as such.

What lunar months and dates are shown in Figures 15 and 16? (Answers on pages 135 and 136.)

Characters to cut out

To learn the characters for numbers, cut out these characters and use them to practice making bigger numbers, months, and dates, as suggested in Chapters 7, 8, and 9. You may wish to glue the characters to heavier paper before cutting them out.

一	一	一	二	二	二
三	三	三	四	四	四
五	五	五	六	六	六
七	七	七	八	八	八
九	九	九	十	十	十
日	日	日	○	○	○
月	月	月	年	年	年

10   十

Positions

The characters for *up*, *down*, and *middle* are very common because of their wide range of meanings and their use in place names. The characters for *left* and *right* are less common.

The position characters are pretty easy to learn:

Up 上 and *down* 下: The lines in 上 go *up* from the floor, and are *above* or *on top of* it. The lines in 下 go *down* from the ceiling, and are *below* or *under* it.

上

左 中 右

下

Middle 中 is symmetrical: The line cuts through the middle of the box.

Left 左 and *right* 右 each represent a hand holding or doing something. The I-shaped part of *left* supposedly represents a carpenter's square, which is held with the left hand. As a separate character, 工, this part means *work* (page 16). The box in *right* is a *mouth* 口 (page 19), since you eat with your right hand. (My apologies to left-handed readers. Feel free to invent your own mnemonics.)

| shàng p.117 | 上 | **upper, above, on, up, ascend, climb, get on** |
| xià p.117 | 下 | **lower, below, under, down, descend, get off** |

zhōng p.121	中	**middle, center, medium**
zuǒ p.124	左	**left, the (political) Left**
yòu p.124	右	**right, the (political) Right**

If you learn only one character from this group, let it be 中. That appears in the name *China*, which is *middle country* 中国 (see page 74).

上 and 下 also appear in place names, the most famous one being Shanghai 上海 (see page 75).

The words 上 and 下, as indicated above, actually cover just about any meaning having to do with being or going up or down. They would be used, for example, for all the italicized words in

I *got on* the bus, which *ascended* a hill.
On top of the hill I *got off* and looked *down*.

FIGURE 17: Great Wall T-shirt

Here the character 上 is used for the verb *climb*.

You might see 上, 中, and 下 on book covers, where they identify the volumes of a two- or three-volume set. 上 is the first volume, 下 is the last, and 中 is the middle (if there are three). (Imagine the books in a stack with the first volume on top.)

Here's another word you wouldn't expect to be made out of position characters:

 approximately

A sign at the Beijing Zoo informed me that the life-span of the Lesser Panda (a raccoon-like animal) can reach 12 年左右 (12 years approximately).

FIGURE 18: From picture captions in a brochure

These labels preceded figure captions in a brochure. Where on the page were the three pictures located? (Note: The : after each label is a colon.) (See page 136 for answer.)

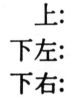

ABOUT CHINESE

Word order. You can make more sense out of what you see if you know a little about word order. Consider the phrases 山上 and 上山.

山上 means *on the mountain* because *on/up* comes after *mountain*. This word order (in which a preposition follows its object) is the opposite of English.

上山 means *climb the mountain* because *climb/up* comes before *mountain*. This word order (in which a verb precedes its object, as with 开门 and 关门 on page 21) is the same as in English.

---

11 十一

Nature

Many of these nature characters are common in place names. (A few such names are shown in Chapter 20.)

FIGURE 19: Nature characters in natural settings

The character for *mountain* 山 is a drawing of a mountain with three peaks:

shān
p.119

山

mountain, hill

There are several words for *river* in Chinese. 川 is nice to know because it appears in the name of Sichuan 四川 province (see page 74). Think of it as a drawing of flowing water, or of two banks with flowing water between them:

chuān
p.114

川

river

I think of *fire* 火 as a person 人 running with his arms up in the air yelling "Help! Fire!"

huǒ
p.118

火

fire

Make up your own mnemonics for the remaining characters.

yún   (s)
p.116

云

cloud

云 is the *yun* of *Yunnan* (see page 74).

shí
p.124

石

stone

Don't confuse *stone* 石 with *right* 右 (page 38). The long stroke in *stone* doesn't stick up as the stroke in *right* does.

stone: 石   right: 右

fēng (s) p.126	风	**wind**
mù p.122	木	**tree, wood**

Two *tree*s combined into a single character make a *forest*:

lín p.122	林	**forest**

林 is the *lin* of *Guilin* (Figure 20 below).

shuǐ p.122	水	**water**

Don't confuse *water* 水 with *tree* 木. Here is a case where knowing how the characters are written will make you aware of what might otherwise be subtle differences in their appearance. The "branches" of the *tree* consist of a single horizontal line, whereas the left and right sides of *water* are drawn separately, with the right-hand "branch" slanting a little.

FIGURE 20: "Guilin"

The first two characters of the map title say *Guilin*. (林 was explained above.)

Notice that the English translation *Chuanshan Hill* says *hill* twice — once in Chinese (*shan*) and once in English.

塔 山
Pagoda Hill

穿 山
Chuanshan Hill

桂林游览示意图
TOURIST SKETCH MAP OF GUILIN

---

sea

海 is one of the most complicated characters in this book. It is included because of its frequent use in place names, such as Shanghai 上海 and Beihai 北海 Park in Beijing. Don't worry about recognizing it out of context: It is usually seen with simpler characters, as in the names just shown. (For these names and others, see Chapter 20.)

Notice the three small lines on the left of 海. (They're easier to see on the handwritten character above.) That set of lines, which is called the *water radical*, appears on the left side of many characters whose meaning has to do with water or other fluids. (See, for example, *steam* in the figures in Chapter 13 and *harbor* in the top figure on page 134.) When you see it, you are pretty safe in guessing that a liquid is involved. In particular, most characters for bodies of water have the water radical. (The *river* character 川 shown above is an exception, though it also has three lines.)

ABOUT CHINESE

Radicals and dictionaries. A traditional Chinese dictionary classifies characters according to about 200 *radicals* — components that appear frequently in characters. Some radicals (such as the *water radical* we saw in 海 above) can only be part of a character, while others can also stand alone (*fire* 火 appears on page 70 both alone and in *smoke*). To look up a character, you have to guess what part of it your dictionary views as the radical, find the radical in a table organized by the number of strokes used to write it, then find the character in that radical's table. Be grateful for alphabets!

Here are some longer words made out of these nature characters:

海 水   **seawater, brine**

海 风   **sea breeze**

山 林   **mountain forest**
(also: wooded mountain,
wooded and hilly lands)

火 山   **volcano**

火 石   **flint**

山 川   **landscape**

山 水   **landscape**
(also: water from
a mountain)

风 水   **geomantic omen,
feng shui** (location of a
house or tomb, supposed
to have an influence on
the fortune of a family —
pronounced *fung shway*)

风 云   **wind & cloud**
(i.e., a stormy or
unstable situation)

FIGURE 21: At a Yunnan scenic attraction

Where was this photograph taken? (Hint: Read from right to left.) (See page 136 for answer.)

ABOUT CHINESE

Direction of writing. Chinese was traditionally written in top-to-bottom *columns*, the columns reading from right to left. Now it is also written in left-to-right *lines*, like English.

Sometimes a name, phrase, or other short (one-line) text is written from right to left, as in the figure above and the top figure on page 104. You will be excited to find that you can sometimes tell when a sign starts on the right. You might recognize a character sequence (such as the name of the city you're in or the word 人民, page 9) that makes sense only in one direction. Or you might realize that the leftmost character is something (such as 店, page 16) that belongs at the end.

12　十二

Electricity

The names of many things that work by electricity start with the character for *electricity*. See, for example, *telephone* and *elevator* on the next page.

diàn　　(s)　　　电　　　**electricity, electric**
p.121

You might think 电 looks like the kite Benjamin Franklin flew in a thunderstorm to demonstrate that lightning is a gigantic electric spark. (Don't try this at home, folks!)

ABOUT CHINESE

Nouns used as adjectives. The form of a Chinese word doesn't depend on its role in the sentence. So you don't have to learn different noun and adjective forms such as *electricity/electric* or *China/Chinese*.

FIGURE 22: Electrical Engineering Department

The EE Department at Xi'an Jiaotong University offers six specialties. Notice that 电 appears in the department name (top line) and in each specialty.

五、电气工程系
1. 电机
2. 电器
3. 工业电气自动化
4. 电力系统及其自动化
5. 高电压技术及设备
6. 电气绝缘与电缆

FIGURE 23: Elevator billboard

This billboard advertises the *Kunming Elevator Factory*. The first two large characters say *Kunming* (you may recognize 明 from page 27), the next two mean *elevator* (literally *electric stairs*), and the last one means *factory* (see page 16).

FIGURE 24: "Public telephone"

The first two characters mean *public* (literally *public use* — see Chapter 16) and the next two mean *telephone* (literally *electric speech*). Compare to phone sign on page 57.

---

13 十三

Vehicles

Vehicle is the final character in the names of many kinds of vehicles. The other parts of some of these names have been shown in earlier chapters.

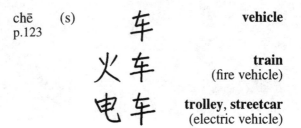

chē (s) p.123	车	**vehicle**
	火车	**train** (fire vehicle)
	电车	**trolley, streetcar** (electric vehicle)

The words for *bus* and *taxi* are four characters long, but you can recognize them easily by their first and last characters.

Taxi (Figure 25) starts with *exit* 出 (page 20) and ends with *vehicle* 车. It means *rent car*.

Bus (Figure 26) starts with *public* 公 (page 56) and ends with *vehicle* 车. It means *public car*.

FIGURE 25: From a taxi receipt

北京市出租汽车

BEIJING TAXI

The first two characters say *Beijing* (page 78), the next one means *city* or *municipal* (page 68), and the last four mean *taxi* (literally *rent car*). A *car* (or *motor vehicle*) is literally a *steam vehicle*.

FIGURE **26**: From the door of a bus

The first two characters say *Beijing* (page 78), the next one means *city* or *municipal* (page 68), and the last four mean *bus* (literally *public car*). A *car* (or *motor vehicle*) is literally a *steam vehicle*.

Try not to be confused by the broken lines in the characters, which result from painting the sign with a stencil. (Notice how easily you can handle the breaks in the numerals underneath.)

14   十四

Hearts and minds

The *heart* in Chinese, like the *heart* in English, is not just a part of the body but also a center of feeling. And, as in English, it can mean *center*.

xīn
p.115

心

heart, mind, feeling, center

Lots of interesting words are made by combining 心 with characters we've seen in earlier chapters. Here are the two you are most likely to see. The first is the *center* in names such as *Shanghai Exhibition Center* or the tea center in the figure on page 77; the second is the *caution* that appears on warning signs.

中心

center
(middle heart)

小心

be careful, caution!
(small heart)

FIGURE 27: A headline in the *Tianjin Daily*

南开大学成立中心实验室

The headline says "Nankai (South Open) University establishes central laboratory." The words *south* 南, *open* 开, and *university* 大学 are taught elsewhere in this book (use the English Word Index to find them). The word *central* is the same as *center* taught above.

Here are some feelings and attitudes, all ending with 心

一 心	**of one mind, wholeheartedly** (one heart/mind)
二 心	**disloyalty, halfheartedness** (two hearts/minds)
安 心	**feel at ease, be relieved** (peaceful heart)
开 心	**feel happy, rejoice, enjoy** (open heart)
关 心	**be concerned with, care for** (close[d] heart)
人 心 or 民 心	**popular feeling, the will of the people** (people feeling)

And here are some more physical things, all starting with 心

心 口	**pit of the stomach** (heart['s] mouth)
心 力	**mental and physical efforts** (heart/mind power)
心 火	**internal heat, hidden anger** (heart/central fire)

"Internal heat" is a concept of Chinese medicine — a disorder whose symptoms include rapid pulse, thirst, and mental uneasiness.

15   十五

Directions

The directions *north*, *south*, *east*, and *west* are used a lot in place names. (See Chapter 20.)

dōng (s) p.123	东		**east**
nán p.126	南		**south**
xī p.121	西		**west**
běi p.117	北		**north**

East becomes easier to remember if you look at its traditional form 東, which looks like the *sun* 日 superimposed on a *tree* 木 (the view you see in the East when the sun is rising). If you remove the angular part of the simplified character 东, it still resembles a 木. Remembering the *tree* component of *east* will also help keep you from confusing *east* with *vehicle* (page 48).

east: 东   vehicle: 车

South is quite complicated, but I couldn't just omit one of the four directions. If you are in a place whose name contains *nan*, you can expect to see 南 in the place name. (Other characters pronounced *nan* are not likely to be used in place names.) See Chapter 20 and the map on page 54 for examples.

West may seem similar to *four*. Since these are both very common characters, you will have many opportunities to learn which is which.

west: 西   four: 四

In English, the four in-between directions start with *north* or *south*. That is, we say *northeast* but never *eastnorth*. In Chinese, the in-between directions start with *east* or *west*, as shown on the compass rose on page 54.

Directions in street names

Street names in China, like those elsewhere, often contain numbers and directions. The direction may come at the beginning of the name, as in *East Five Road* in Xi'an, or after the main part of the name, as in *People's South Road* in Chengdu (shown in the figure on page 10). As you travel north on 人民南 (*People's South*) Road, its name changes first to 人民中 (*People's Middle*) Road and then to 人民北 (*People's North*) Road.

Western versus Chinese

West 西 is used a lot to distinguish western things from Chinese things — for example, western food, western medicine. (In this sense it could also be translated as *occidental*.) And it is used in names of many things that come from the West, such as watermelon (western melon) and tomato (western red persimmon).

Similarly, *middle* 中 (page 38) is used to identify Chinese things — for example, Chinese food, Chinese medicine. Why *middle*? Because the name of China is *middle country* 中国 (see map on page 54).

FIGURE 28: Compass directions in China

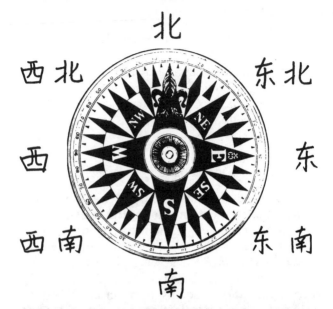

北

西北　　　　东北

西　　　　　　东

西南　　　　东南

南

CHINA 中国

YUNNAN
云南

When a direction is not a direction

The third character of *Mao Zedong* is *east* 东. (See the stamp on page 104.)

There are no such directions as *east-west* or *west-west*, but those combinations are words:

 thing

 cc, cubic centimeter

西 西, pronounced *xīxī*, sounds like *cc* ("see-see") in English. Do you think it's an accident that 西 was chosen for this western measurement from the many sound-alike characters?

FIGURE 29: Caption on a postcard

东汉石刻李冰像
Stone statue of Li Bing

The character *east* at the beginning of the Chinese caption is part of *Eastern Han* (a dynasty, A.D.25-220). The rest of the caption has the same meaning in Chinese and English. (You might recognize *stone*, from page 41.)

Quite a few names of Chinese dynasties have directions in them. The direction in a name refers to the location of the dynasty's capital.

---

16 十六

Public things

Public is common in several contexts, as we will see below.

gōng
p.116

公 or 公

public, metric

Notice that the two forms of the top of *public* are the same as the two forms of *eight*, shown on page 23. The first form of *public* is the normal handwritten form; the second is common in printed matter.

公 is the first character of *bus* (*public car* — see page 48).

It combines with characters for *manage* 司, *use* 用, and *park* 园 to form common words, as follows:

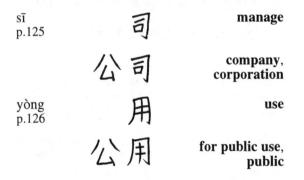

sī
p.125

司

manage

公司

company, corporation

yòng
p.126

用

use

公用

for public use, public

You will see 公用 on *public telephone* signs (as in the figure opposite).

yuán (s) **park, garden**
p.121

园 is the end of the words for many kinds of places for public recreation and places where plants are grown. For example, it is the last character in *zoo* (animal park), *flower garden*, and *orchard* (fruit garden). The most common such place is

 public park

You will see 公园 in the names of many parks, such as Beihai Park in Beijing (page 76). A very popular name for parks is

人民公园 **People's Park**

FIGURE 30: From a taxi receipt

友 谊 出 租 汽 车 公 司
FRIENDSHIP TAXI COMPANY

The first two characters mean *friendship*. *Taxi* (the middle four characters) is explained in Chapter 13.

FIGURE 31: "Public telephone"

The last two characters mean *telephone* (see Chapter 12). Compare to phone sign on page 47.

The last large character in this sign, *park* 园, was shown above. The character before it, which has a field 田 (page 11) on the top and a tree 木 (page 42) on the bottom, means *fruit*. *Fruit park* means *orchard*.

Dates and Metric measurements

公 is also used in some systems of measurement imported from abroad. It is the first character of

> some units of measure in the metric system (see Figure 33)

> words that identify a date as A.D. or B.C. (see Figure 34)

> the word that marks a date as Gregorian rather than lunar (see Figure 35)

I will not show you the metric units. When you expect to see a measurement and you see a number followed by something starting with the character 公 for *metric*, it will usually be obvious from the con-

---

text what the unit is. For example, if the price on a roll of fabric has 公 after it, it must be the price per meter of fabric. (If you find someone selling fabric by the kilometer or the gram, let me know!) Unfortunately, not every metric measurement contains 公, since some of the units have alternate names.

FIGURE 33: From a taxi receipt

The last two characters mean *kilometer*.

行驶公里
Drive Kilometres

FIGURE 34: A.D. and B.C. dates from a pamphlet

明嘉靖三十九年

（公元一五六〇年）。

公元前二一九年

In the top line a date is given in traditional Chinese style, as the *thirty-ninth year* of the reign of an emperor in the *Ming* 明 dynasty (first comes the dynasty, then the emperor, then the year). Then, in parentheses, the equivalent year *A.D.1560* is shown. The first two characters in the parentheses mean *A.D.*, and the rest give the year (see Chapter 9).

The bottom line shows the date *219 B.C.* The first three characters, which mean *B.C.*, are the same as the word *A.D.* (directly above) followed by a character meaning *before*.

You'll meet 元 again in the next chapter, with a different meaning.

FIGURE 35: Gregorian and lunar dates

公历5月5日　农历三月二十

This line from a 1988 calendar shows that in that year, the Gregorian date May 5 fell on the 20th day of the 3rd lunar month. The two characters preceding each date tell which calendar system is being used. The first one says *Gregorian* (literally *public*) *calendar*; the second says *lunar* (literally *farm*) *calendar*.

17　十七

Money

You can handle Chinese money without knowing any characters, because the denominations of all but a few bills and coins are shown in arabic numerals and Pinyin. (And the few that don't have numerals and Pinyin are worth so little that it hardly matters if you mix them up.) But you might like to be familiar with at least one simple money-related character.

The basic unit of Renminbi (*the people's* 人民 *currency*, abbreviated RMB) is the *yuan*, analogous to the U.S. dollar.

yuán p.116	元	**yuan, dollar**

In fact, 元 is the translation of *dollar* for any currency that uses dollars (e.g., Canadian, U.S.).

元 is also the *yuan* of the *Yuan* (or Mongol) dynasty (1271-1368), which started with Kublai Khan's rule and was followed by the *Ming* 明 dynasty.

The *yuan* is divided into 100 *fen* (analogous to U.S. pennies). 10 *fen* make 1 *jiao* (analogous to a U.S. dime). The characters for *fen* and *jiao* are shown in Figures 36-39 on the following pages.

Prices

Prices are normally given as a number of yuan, but small prices may be given as a number of jiao or fen. These are analogous to prices given in dollars (e.g., $2.50) or in cents (e.g., 50¢).

FIGURE 36: Bottom edges of stamps

Next to the stamp values (*1.10 yuan* and *70 fen*) it says *China People's Postal Service.*

FIGURE 37: 5-jiao and 2-yuan admission tickets

The large characters on the lefthand ticket say *five jiao,* and the large characters on the righthand ticket say *two yuan.* You won't recognize these words for *two* and *five,* because they are the complex characters used on currency (see opposite). But you can see an ordinary *five* 五 embedded in this *five.*

The symbol ¥ is not a Chinese character. It is analogous to a dollar sign ($).

For more examples of prices in jiao and fen, see the tickets on page 107.

ABOUT CHINESE

Phonetic information in characters. Notice that 元 is the same as the inside part of *park* 园 (page 57), and that both of these characters are pronounced *yuán*. A 园 is something with a boundary (the box) that is pronounced like 元. The outside of 园 tells something about its meaning and the inside tells something about its sound.

Although you have learned lots of characters derived from pictures of things (such as 人 and 田) or from symbolic representations of abstract concepts (such as 一 and 上), and several characters made from two characters that contribute meanings (such as 明), it turns out that most Chinese characters are like 园. That is, most characters contain a part that hints at the meaning and a part that hints at the sound. (The phonetic information, like that in English spelling, is often only approximate due to pronunciation changes over time.)

For another phonetic example, look at the name *Kodak* in the sign on page 18. The first character, pronounced kē, contains 可 (page 71), which is pronounced kě. The second character, pronounced dá, contains 大 (page 14), which is pronounced dà.

Understanding the value of money

The ordinary numbers we learned in Chapter 7 are not used in finance because they are too easy to modify. (Just think how simple it would be to turn a *one* 一 into a *ten* 十 on a check!) Instead, complex characters are used. (See the left-hand large character on each bill in the following figures.) But you needn't learn these characters or those for *fen*, *jiao*, or *yuan* (also shown in the figures): Except on fen bills, the value is also given in numerals, and any coin or bill that doesn't say *jiao* or *yuan* is *fen*.

FIGURE 38: 1-fen and 2-fen bills

The right-hand large character on each bill is *fen*, and the left-hand character is the number of fen. On a fen bill, there are no numerals or Pinyin. You can compare the left-hand character to those on jiao or yuan bills, which also have numerals, to see which is which. Or you can think up a way to remember that the truck is 1 and the airplane is 2 (for example: 1 comes before 2 and the truck was invented before the airplane; or the truck has 1 engine and the airplane has 2).

FIGURE 39: 1-jiao and 5-jiao bills

The large character on the upper right of each bill is *jiao*.

FIGURE 40: 1-yuan and 2-yuan bills

On money, a more complicated character than the 元 introduced on page 61 is used for *yuan*. (See the large character at the upper right of each bill.) But don't worry: "*yuan*" appears elsewhere on the bill.

18 十八

King and country

Nation 国 is the last character of some country names, including China (middle country) and the United States (beautiful country). It is also part of words relating to nations, such as *international*.

guó (s)	国	**country,**
p.120		**nation, national**

Let's take a closer look at the inside of 国

yù	玉	**jade**
p.115		

which can also be combined with *stone* 石 (page 41)

玉 石 **jade**

and which is just a little bit different from another valuable thing:

wáng	王	**king**
p.115		

Wang, also spelled *Wong* (which better indicates the English pronunciation) outside China, is a common surname (see figure opposite).

Here's another word for *king*:

国 王 **king**

You might remember 玉 as the 王 holding his jade seal, and 国 as valuable things (such as 玉) contained within a national boundary.

After the Han dynasty broke up in A.D.220, China was divided into

 Three Kingdoms

ABOUT CHINESE

People's names. A Chinese name is usually two or three syllables, of which the first is the surname. For example: Mao Zedong (surname Mao), Deng Xiaoping (surname Deng). If Chinese people move to a country where surnames come last, they generally move their surname to the end to avoid confusion.

FIGURE 41: Names on a theater program

These staff members worked behind the scenes at a theater. The boldface words at the left are the kinds of job (lighting, makeup, and so on) and the words to the right of the colons are the people's names. You will find familiar characters (3 from this chapter and 5 from other chapters) in 14 of the 17 names shown here (out of the original 26 names). How many of these people have the surname *Wang*? (Answer on page 136.)

工 作 人 员 表

钢琴伴奏：刘小明　王　敏

灯　光：冯胜国　王椿铭　胡永昌　王永德

装　置：方盛华　乔正荣　李雪山　彭建国

服　装：叶玉英　王嘉麟　郭小红

音　响：沈华云　王永大

化　妆：浦国敏　金玉英

Logical order of names, addresses, and dates.
Dates, addresses, and people's names all start with
the largest or most general part, then progress to
successively more specific parts. Dates have the
year first, then the month, and finally the day.
Addresses have the country before the city before
the street before the number. People's names have
the surname before the given name.

The next character often appears after a city
name, with its *municipal* meaning. It may also appear on stores with its *market* meaning.

shì p.127		**city**, **municipal[ity]**, **market**

市 is also the first character of some traditional
Chinese units of measure. I don't know how likely
you are to see this usage, as the metric system is
widely used in China today.

FIGURE 42: Great Wall ticket

The first two
characters say
Beijing (page
78).

19　十九

Prohibition or permission?

If you see one of these characters on a sign, the sign may be prohibiting something — for example: *No smoking*, *Photography forbidden*, *Do not enter*.

bù
p.117

不

no, not, un-, …
(不 corresponds to many negative prefixes in English.)

jīn
p.122

禁

prohibit, forbid

Don't be scared off too easily by the complexity of this character. Sometimes a complex character is not hard to recognize. 禁, for example, is symmetrical. And its top half 林 may look familiar from page 42: As a separate character, it means *forest*. The bottom half looks to me like the character for *no* shown above. It's actually not the same, as you can see if you look carefully. But thinking of it as *no* helps me remember that 禁 is the other negative character I know.

FIGURE 43: "Unknown year Yunnan pu-er" tea

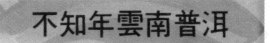

In addition to the *un* of *unknown*, you may recognize *year* and *south* (*nan*). This tea can, intended for export, uses the traditional *cloud* character for *yun* in *Yunnan*.

FIGURE 44: "No smoking" sign

The first two characters mean *prohibited*; the last two mean *smoking*. Notice the character *fire* 火 on the left side of the last character. When 火 is part of a larger character it is called the *fire radical*. The fire radical appears on the left side of many characters having to do with fire (such as words for lamp, stove, kitchen, and fry).

FIGURE 45: "No smoking or fires"

The first two characters of this sign mean *strictly forbidden*, the next two mean *smoke* (same as in Figure 44), and the last two mean *light a fire*. There's a comma between *smoke* and *light a fire*.

Here's a more positive character:

kě
p.125

可 **may**, **can**

But be sure to notice what's in front of it:

不可 **cannot**, **must not**, **should not**

You might confuse *can* with *manage* (page 56) if you saw the characters alone:

can: 可 manage: 司

But in real life you can tell the characters apart from the context, because you are unlikely to see *manage* 司 except in the word *company*, where it is preceded by 公 (see page 56).

可 in foreign words

You'll probably see 可 being used to transliterate the sound *co* in foreign words, such as *Coca-Cola* and *cocoa*.

It's hard to spend more than a few minutes in China without encountering Coca-Cola. And if, like me, you don't drink tea or beer, you may find yourself subsisting on Coke even if you never drink it at home.

Take a look at the cans on page 73. You probably recognize the second character, 口, of *Coca-Cola*, which means *mouth* (page 19). The first and third characters are 可, introduced above. We won't study the fourth character, which means *enjoy*.

All together, the name is *kě kǒu kě lè*. This was chosen both to sound similar to *Coca-Cola* and to have an appropriate meaning. If you look only at the sound, the choice of name seems strange: The second syllable (*kǒu*) of the Chinese sounds just like the first and third syllables (*Co*) of the English, and the first and third syllables of the Chinese (*kě*) sound like the second syllable (*ca*) of the English. So why didn't they instead call the product *kǒu kě kǒu lè*, which would sound almost exactly like *Coca-Cola*? Probably because the chosen distortion of the sound produces the meaning "tasty, can enjoy."

可 口   **tasty** (can/may mouth)

Here is another foreign sweet whose name uses the character 可.

可 可   **cocoa**

I don't know how the name 可可, pronounced *kěkě*, was chosen from various possibilities that would sound similar to *cocoa*. Perhaps it makes chocoholics feel good by giving us permission to indulge.

FIGURE 46: Chocolate-bar wrapper

Notice the word *cocoa*, which appears twice.

成　份：可可豆，可可脂，奶粉，砂糖，磷脂，香兰素和桂皮。

INGREDIENTS: Cocoa Beans, Cocoa Butter, Powdered Milk, Sugar, Lecithin, Vanillin and Cinnamon.

FIGURE 47: Coca-Cola in China

One view of a Coca-Cola can.

The writing on the other side of the can. (See page 136 for explanation of some characters.)

可口可乐
中国第六届运动会
指定可乐型饮料

The official Cola beverage of the 6th National Games, PRC

When our tour group made a rest stop at a Yi-minority village on the Burma Road in Yunnan, this child was happy to share our Coke.

Place names

If you don't know any spoken Chinese, it may be hard to learn place names. You may recognize the characters making up the name (hence the meaning of the name) but not know what name it is. For example, you may recognize 西安 as *western peace* without realizing that it is the city *Xi'an*. If you visit a place, however, you will probably see its name quite a lot, and it may become easy to recognize.

Many place names contain characters you've seen in this book. In fact, about 2/3 of the places for which there are entries in my copy of *The China Guidebook* contain one or more of "your" characters in their names.

Here are some names made entirely out of characters from earlier chapters. Two of these names appear on the map on page 54.

| Zhōngguó | | **China** (middle country) |

The full name *People's Republic of China* is shown in Figure 48. (Unfortunately, it doesn't contain this word 中国 for *China*; it consists of the characters 中 and 国 with five other characters between them.)

| **Sìchuān** (province) | 四 川 | (four rivers) |
| **Yúnnán** (province) | 云 南 | (cloud south = south of the clouds) |

Shāndōng (province)	山东	(mountain east = east of the mountain)
Shānxī (province)	山西	(mountain west = west of the mountain)
Xī'ān (city)	西安	(western peace)
Shànghǎi (city)	上海	(up sea)

Although the second character of *Shanghai* may be hard to remember, you'll find it easy to recognize together with the first character — especially if you are expecting to see it because you are in Shanghai.

Hǎinán (island)	海南	(sea south = south of the sea)

If you want to know what body of water 海南 island is located in, just write it backwards:

Nánhǎi	南海	**South China Sea** (south sea)

Here are the Chinese names for some other seas:

Dōnghǎi	东海	**East China Sea** (east sea)
Běihǎi	北海	**North Sea**

Note that the 北海 is in Europe, not near China. Surprisingly, 北海 is also the name of a town in southern China, only about 100 miles from Vietnam.

Here are some famous places in Beijing:

Tiān'ānmén 天安门 (heavenly peace gate)

北海公园 **Beihai Park** (north sea park)

Zhōngnánhǎi (government compound) 中南海 (middle south sea = middle & south seas)

北海公园 is just north of 中南海. In these names, 海 refers to a lake rather than a sea.

Some city names that contain only one character from this book — including Kunming, Tianjin, and Guilin — are shown in Figures 3 (page 15), 7 (page 18), 20 (page 42), 23 (page 47), and 58 (page 101).

FIGURE 48: Tian'anmen

This large sign on Tian'anmen 天安门 says *Long live the People's Republic of China*. The first seven characters are *People's Republic of China*. The expression *long live* is literally *10,000* (second to last character) *years old* (last character).

FIGURE 49: "Yunnan," simplified and traditional

云 南 省 茶 叶 贸 易 中 心
雲南省茶叶进出口公司谨制

Both of these lines from a set of Yunnan teas start with *Yunnan province tea* (literally *tea leaf*), but the top line uses the simplified *cloud* and the bottom line uses the traditional *cloud*. The bottom line ("made by Yunnan province tea import-export corporation") was on the outside of the package, and the top line ("Yunnan province tea trade center") was on the individual tea boxes inside the package. The words *Yunnan*, *export*, *corporation*, and *center* are taught in this book.

Directions in place names

Many place names contain *north* 北 (bei), *south* 南 (nan), *east* 东 (dong), or *west* 西 (xi). In fact, the names of about half of China's provinces end with a direction: Hénán, Héběi, Húnán, Húběi, Jiāngxī, Guǎngdōng, Shāndōng, Shānxī, Shǎnxī,* Yúnnán.

Notice how the meaning depends on whether the direction is first or second in the name. In *Xi'an* the direction comes first, so it modifies the rest of the name — hence the meaning "western peace." But in *Shandong* the direction is at the end, so it refers to that direction from the rest of the name — hence the meaning "east of the mountain."

Directions are also common in street names (see page 53).

---

* Don't confuse Shānxī province (spelled *Shanxi* when tone marks are omitted) with Shǎnxī province (spelled *Shaanxi* when tone marks are omitted, to distinguish it from *Shanxi*). Xī'ān is the capital of Shǎnxī (Shaanxi).

Names with "jing" or "zhou"

The old word 京 for *capital* isn't used today for capital cities, but it is the second character of *Beijing* (China's capital) and *Nanjing* (a former capital).

jīng p.123	京	**capital** (of a country)
Běijīng	北京	(north capital)
Nánjīng	南京	(south capital)

One of the many famous universities in China is

北京大学　**Beijing University**

which is often abbreviated to

北大　**Beijing U.**

Lots of place names in China — such as Suzhou, Hangzhou, and Guangzhou (Canton) — end with the character 州, which no longer has a meaning. (*Zhou* was spelled *chow* before the adoption of Pinyin. It is pronounced *Joe*.)

zhōu p.114	州	(no current meaning)

If you are in a place whose name ends with *zhou* and you see 州, you can assume that it is the end of that name. The preceding characters, one per syllable, form the rest of the name (see Figure 54).

Notice how 州 differs from *river* 川 (see *Sichuan* on page 74).

The inhabitants

In English, we have various ways of identifying a person from a particular place. We may be able to add one of a few standard suffixes to the place name (New Yorker, Bostonian, etc.) or we may have to use a special word (such as Cantabrigian*).

The Chinese have a simpler way of handling this. Just put *person* 人 after the name of the place:

中国人   **Chinese person**

上海人   **Shanghai person**

Sun Yat-sen

Sun Yat-sen's name is popular as a place name in China, as George Washington's is in the U.S. Sun Yat-sen was also known as Sun Zhongshan,** and is generally referred to today as just

Zhōngshān   中山   **Sun Yat-sen** (middle mountain)

My guidebook shows three cities with a Sun Yat-sen Park or Zhongshan Park.

中山公园   **Sun Yat-sen Park** (middle mountain park)

---

* A person from Cambridge, Massachusetts
** He was originally named Sun Wen, but changed his name to Sun Yat-sen when he was baptized. While living in Japan, he used the common Japanese name Nakayama, which means *middle mountain* and is written 中山, hence pronounced *Zhongshan* in Chinese.

FIGURE 50: From a tourist map of Taiwan

中山高速公路

SUN YAT-SEN FREEWAY

A *freeway* is a *high speed public road*. You know the character for *public* (page 56). This same character for *road* also appears on the postcard on page 10.

FIGURE 51: Address on a menu

Where is this restaurant located? The two characters before the colon say *address*. The last character means *inside*. (Answer on page 136.)

地址： 北海公园内

FIGURE 52: License plates

License plates have the province or, in the case of several major cities (Beijing, Shanghai, and Tianjin), the city. Can you identify these? (Answer on page 136.)

FIGURE 53: Luggage tags

The left-hand tag says *Kunming*. What other city did I fly to? (Answer on page 136.)

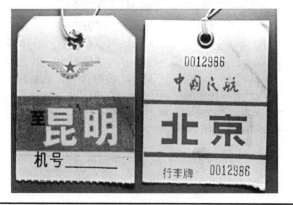

FIGURE 54: Boarding passes

The top boarding pass says *Guangzhou* (Canton). What is the destination on the other boarding pass? (Answer on page 136.)

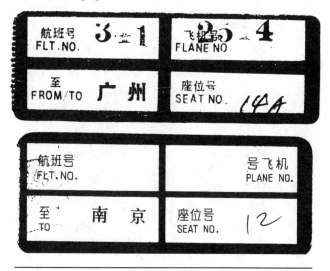

21 二十一

Some words and phrases

Here are some words and phrases that combine characters from earlier chapters. (Not all of these examples are common: They're here for practice.) Cover up the English and see if you can guess what they mean. You can use the literal meaning to look up the characters in the English Word Index.

中 人   middleman,
go-between, mediator
[middle person]

大 人   grownup
[big person]

Unfortunately, in China you will see a more complicated word corresponding to *adult* on ticket price lists rather than this informal word. 大人, like *grownup* in English, is used mostly by children.

工 人   worker
[work person]

人 工   artificial, man-made
[person work]

木 工   carpenter, carpentry
[wood work(er)]

石 工   mason, masonry
[stone work(er)]

电 工   electrician
[electricity worker]

月	工	laborer hired by the month [month worker]
日	工	day laborer [day worker]
民	工	laborer working on a public project [people worker]
小	工	unskilled laborer [small worker]
山	田	hillside plot [mountain field]
水	田	paddy [water field]
田	园	fields & gardens, countryside [field garden]
口	水	saliva [mouth water]
山	口	mountain pass [mountain mouth/opening]
火 山	口	crater [volcano (fire mountain) mouth/opening]
海	口	seaport [sea mouth/opening]
风	口	a place where there is a draft [wind mouth/opening]

人 口　population
[person mouth]

In English we also sometimes count people by their mouths, as when we speak of the number of mouths to feed.

一 口　a bite, mouthful
[one mouth]

一 二　one or two,
just a little, just a few
[one two]

大 风　gale, strong wind
[big wind]

东 风　east wind, the East Wind

"The East Wind" is the driving force of revolution. It is thus popular in names — for example, a Beijing market and a Chengdu hotel.

上 风　windward, upwind
[up wind]

下 风　leeward, downwind
[down wind]

上 司　superior, boss
[upper/above manage]

小 国　small country

王 国　kingdom, realm, domain
[king nation]

Do you remember 国 王 from page 66?

女 王　queen
[female king]

天 国　　　　paradise (Kingdom
　　　　　　　　　　of Heaven)
　　　　　　　　　[heaven nation]

天 下　　　　the whole world, or China
　　　　[heaven under = under heaven]

There is a beautiful book of photographs by
Eliot Porter (with text by Jonathan Porter)
called *All Under Heaven: The Chinese World.*
The first section, called "All Under Heaven:
Tianxia," explains the use and implications of
the word *tianxia* 天下 over a couple of
millennia.

天 明　　　　　daybreak, dawn
　　　　　　　　　[sky/day bright]

Do you remember what 明天 means (see page
27)?

明 年　　　　　　　　next year
　　　　　　　　　　　[bright year]

明 月　　　　　　　　bright moon

I apologize for the fact that 明月 doesn't mean
next month.

水 门　　　　　　　　water valve
　　　　　　　　　　　[water gate]

电 门　　　　　　　electric switch
　　　　　　　　　[electricity gate]

Do you remember the other word for *switch*?

天 电　　　atmospheric electrical
　　　　　　　disturbances, static
　　　　　　　　　[sky electricity]

电 力　　　　　　　electric power

风	力		wind power
国	力		national power
火	力		firepower (military)
水	力		water (hydraulic) power
水	力	学	hydraulics [hydraulic (water) power study]
电	学		electricity (as a science) [electricity study]
人	力	车	rickshaw [person power vehicle]
工	力		skill, craftsmanship [work ability]
用	力		to exert oneself [use strength/ability]
用	心		diligently, attentively [use mind/heart]
学	年		school year
入	学		to start school [enter school]
不	小心		careless [not careful (small heart)]

不 可 入 口　　　not to be taken orally
　　　　　　　　　　　[not can enter mouth]

中 年　　　　　　　　　　middle age
　　　　　　　　　　　　　[middle year]

中 年 人　　　　middle-aged person
　　　　　　　　　[middle year person]

月 中　　　　　　middle of a month
　　　　　　　　　　[month middle]

市 中 心　　　city center, downtown
　　　　　[city center (middle heart)]

市 民　　　　　　　　townspeople,
　　　　　　　　residents of a city
　　　　　　　　　[city people/folk]

小 市 民　　　urban petty bourgeois
　　　　　　[small city people/folk]

公 民　　　　　　　　　　citizen
　　　　　　　　　　　[public folk]

公 开　　　　　overt, open, public,
　　　　　　　　　to make public
　　　　　　　　　　[public open]

公 安　　　　　　public security
　　　　　　　　　　[public peace]

You may see 公安 on signs such as parking
regulations promulgated by a *public security
bureau.*

公 海　　　　　　　　　high seas
　　　　　　　　　　　[public sea]

海 上
at sea
[sea on = on the sea]

This is *Shànghǎi* (page 75) written backwards.

人 海
sea of people,
huge crowd
[person sea]

I'm sorry, but 人海 written backwards is not a word (a *sailor* is not a *sea person*).

人 山 人 海
sea of people,
huge crowd
[person mountain person sea]

I was very excited to be able to read a whole example sentence

in *Fun With Chinese Characters* (see footnote for translation*).

林 海
vast stretch of forest
[forest sea]

山 南 海 北
far and wide
[mountain south sea north = S of the mountains and N of the seas]

海 关
customs
[sea close]

日 出
sunrise
[sun exit]

出 厂
(of products) to leave the factory
[exit factory]

---

* "The train is crowded with people" ("train on huge crowd").

		to produce, manufacture [produce products]
出	品	
出	国	to go abroad [exit nation]
开	口	to open one's mouth, start to talk [open mouth]
开	山	to cut into a mountain (e.g., for quarrying) [open mountain]
开	国	to found a state [open nation]
不	一	to vary, differ [not one]
不 三 不 四		nondescript, neither fish or fowl [not three not four]

Some places

Don't worry about the Pinyin spelling of these place names, just translate the characters into English.

中	东	the Middle East
西	山	Western Hills (in Kunming)
水 上 公 园		Park on the Water (in Tianjin) [water on park (public park)]

Repeating oneself

Here are some two-syllable words made by repeating a character. You may remember some of them from earlier chapters.

In these examples, the repetition of a noun gives the meaning of "every":

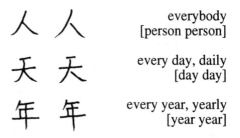

人 人　everybody
　　　　[person person]

天 天　every day, daily
　　　　[day day]

年 年　every year, yearly
　　　　[year year]

In the following words, the repetition of an adjective produces an adverb:

大 大　greatly
　　　　[big big]

明 明　clearly, obviously
　　　　[clear clear]

In some cases, the syllables are used for foreign sounds:

kěkě　可 可　cocoa
　　　　　[can/may can/may]

xīxī　西 西　cc, cubic centimeter
　　　　　[west west]

Combinations of opposites

Often two characters with opposite meanings are combined to indicate one thing "and" the other, or "from" one "to" the other:

男	女	men and women [male female]
中	西	Chinese and Western [middle/China West]
南	北	north and south, from north to south [south north]
东	西	east and west, from east to west [east west]
大	小	big or small [big small]
左	右	left and right sides [left right]

The last three combinations also have special meanings. Do you remember them? If not, look on pages 55, 14, and 39.

The other combination of opposites we saw earlier (page 20) has only one meaning:

开	关	switch [turn on, turn off]

Puzzles

Try these miniature crossword puzzles to see what words you can recognize. I supply the filled-in puzzle, you supply the English definitions for the words that read across and down. All 71 characters taught in this book appear in the puzzles. You can use the Quick Reference to look up characters.

To check your answers, turn to page 137.

Puzzle 1

Puzzle 2

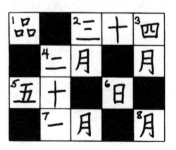

Across	Down
1.	2.
2.	3.
3.	4.
4.	5.
6.	

Across	Down
1.	2.
2.	3.
4.	4.
5.	
6.	
7.	
8.	

Puzzle 3

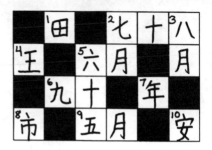

Puzzle 4

Puzzle 5

Across	Down
1.	2.
2.	3.
4.	5.
5.	
6.	
7.	
8.	
9.	
10.	

Across	Down
1.	1.
2.	2.
4.	3.
5.	5.
7.	6.
8.	

Across	Down
1.	1.
3.	2.
4.	3.
7.	5.
8.	6.

Puzzle 6

Puzzle 7

Puzzle 8

(For a hint,
see bottom
of page 98.)

Across	Down
2.	1.
4.	3.
5.	6.
7.	7.
9.	8.
10.	9.
11.	10.

Across	Down
1.	1.
2.	2.
3.	3.
4.	4.
6.	5.
7.	

Across	Down
1.	1.
3.	2.
5.	4.
8.	6.
	7.

Puzzle 9

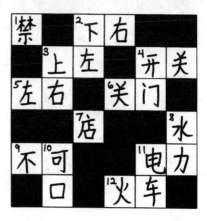

Puzzle 10

(For a hint, see bottom of page.)

Hints

    Puzzle 8 contains a place name.

    Puzzle 10 contains names.

Across	Down
1.	2.
2.	3.
3.	4.
4.	8.
5.	9.
6.	10.
7.	11.
9.	12.
11.	
12.	

Across	Down
1.	2.
3.	4.
4.	6.
5.	8.
7.	9.
8.	11.
9.	
10.	
11.	

23   二十三

Reading practice

Try to recognize characters in these pictures. You can use the Quick Reference to look up characters. Explanations begin on page 140.

FIGURE 55: A sign

What does this sign say? For a hint, see the footnote.*

小火
心车

FIGURE 56: Admission prices

For what category of people is the admission price ¥0.20元?

中国公民	¥0.20元
外国游人	¥1.00元
儿童 1.2米以下	¥0.10元

---

* Figure 55 hint: Read from top to bottom.

FIGURE 57: In London's Heathrow airport

This sign accompanied a display of toiletries in a duty-free shop. What does it say?

FIGURE 58: Table of distances

This table gives the distance from Kunming to twelve other places in 云南 province. What province is that? How far is it from Kunming to the Stone Forest? Can you find familiar characters in five other destinations?

昆明—大理	400 公里
昆明—丽江	600 公里
昆明—中甸	706 公里
昆明—楚雄	185 公里
昆明—曲靖	156 公里
昆明—石林	126 公里
昆明—思茅	580 公里
昆明—景洪	742 公里
昆明—保山	593 公里
昆明—瑞丽	918 公里
昆明—通海	143 公里
昆明—元谋	201 公里

FIGURE 59: A receipt

Where on this receipt would you fill in each part of the date? What kind of institution issued the receipt? In what city? In which column did they write down what I bought?

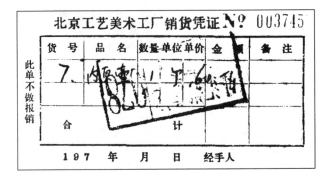

FIGURE 60: Wrapping paper from a souvenir

What kind of institution did I shop at? What material do they work with?

FIGURE 61: Fragment of a CAAC plane ticket

What is the weight limit for luggage on this flight? For a hint, see the footnote.*

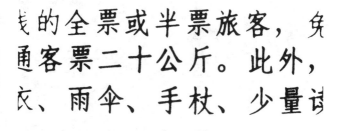

的全票或半票旅客，免
通客票二十公斤。此外，
衣、雨伞、手杖、少量诗

FIGURE 62: From a brochure cover

What is this institution, and where is it located? You may recognize all but the fourth character, and four of the five two-character words.

西北工业大学
中国 · 西安

* Figure 61 hint: Read three consecutive characters.

FIGURE 63: A removable plate in the sidewalk

Read seven of these twelve characters. How can you tell that this reads from right to left?

FIGURE 64: Stamp showing Mao as a young man

Where does the stamp say *Mao Zedong*? (Hint: *dong* is *east*.) What anniversary of his birth is being commemorated?

FIGURE 65: From a brochure

From the first two lines of text in this brochure about the terra cotta army of emperor Qin Shi Huang, try to answer these questions:

When was the buried army discovered?

What city is it near, and in what direction from the city?

What landscape feature is it near, and where is it in relation to that feature?

一九七四年三月，
西安城东的骊山脚下，
模巨大的秦代陶俑坑。

FIGURE 66: Part of a business card

Find the cable number and telephone number on this business card. (If you're not sure which is which, look at the telephone sign on page 47.) Identify the parts of the address, and read as many as six characters in the address.

西安市小寨东路三号
电话：五三九六六
电报挂号：一三五五

FIGURE 67: A children's ride in Beijing

Each line of this sign in Purple Bamboo Park tells you one thing about the ride.

Which line describes the type of ride?

How many people can ride at once?

How much does the ride cost?

How many times can you go around the track for that price?

小羊拉车
每次转绕三圈
票价：一元
（可乘二人）

FIGURE 68: A ticket

Who issued this ticket? You may be able to read the entire top line.

FIGURE 69: Another ticket

What city issued this ticket? Can you guess what it is for? For a hint, see the footnote.*

* Figure 69 hint: Look only at the simplest characters in the top line. The city name is two characters, and two other characters will help you answer the other question.

When and from where was each of these newspaper articles filed? Each of the three fragments contains a boldface dateline in which you can find a date preceded by the name of a city.

新華社上海四月二十四日電 (訊
學全) 一支二萬人的"科技扶貧"隊
上海市科協組織下,目前正活躍在江
浙(江)、滬的中小企業, 幫助開發新
和新產品, 給企業注入了新的活力。
　　最近上海市科協召開的經驗交流

法門寺對外開方

本報西安四月二十四日電 記者
政府最近宣佈, 舉世矚目的法門寺對
塔地宮出土文物將在西安舉行首次展
　　去年四月, 考古工作者在扶風法

中國農村函大建校三

本報北京四月二十二日訊 記者三
中國科協創辦的中國農村致富技術函扗

FIGURE 71: A sign

What does the bottom line of this sign say? For a hint, see the footnote.*

保 护 草 坪
严 禁 入 内

FIGURE 72: Battery

This is the label on a battery from the panda I bought in China. What do you think it says? Try to recognize four of the five characters on the bottom line.

---

* Figure 71 hint: Read the two middle characters.

Does the Chinese match the English?

One thing you can do with your newfound ability to recognize characters is try to decide whether the English and the Chinese say the same thing, in cases where both languages are used. See what evidence you can find in the following examples.

FIGURE 73: Sign at the Great Wall at Mutianyu

The English may be a little hard to read here. It says "No smoking in the mountains !"

FIGURE 74: m&m's® billboard in Beijing

In this case there is no English, but you know that it would say "Melts in your mouth, not in your hand."

FIGURE 75: Caption on a postcard

南京中山陵　　陵门

Mausoleum gate

Sun Yat-sen Mausoleum, Nanjing

FIGURE 76: A book about Tibet

西藏人谈西藏（英）

中国建设出版社出版

Tibetans on Tibet

Published by China Reconstructs Press, Beijing, China

Sometimes you can learn new characters by assuming that the Chinese and the English match. For example, if you notice the parallel structure of the two phrases in Figure 74 and recognize the character for *mouth*, you might assume (correctly) that the last character means *hand*.

Of course, you can be fooled when the Chinese and English are close but not identical, as I was by the postcard on page 30. The postcard says in English "Postcard People's Republic of China." Since I was able to recognize *China People* (first four characters) and *postcard* (last three characters), I mistakenly assumed that the two characters in between meant *Republic*.

24 二十四

How to write characters

This chapter shows how to write the characters taught in this book. Each character is preceded by its main English meaning and by the page number on which it was fully explained. The characters do not appear in the order in which they were introduced in the book — rather, they are grouped according to how they are written.

Stroke order and direction

A character is written with one or more strokes of the pen. In this chapter, small numbers next to a character show the order of the strokes and small arrows show the direction of the strokes.

Two general rules will tell you the direction of all but a few strokes in Chinese characters:

If a line is mostly horizontal, draw it from left to right.

If a line is mostly vertical, draw it from top to bottom.

Stroke order is a little more complicated. Though a few guidelines such as

   top before bottom

   left before right

will help you guess or remember the stroke order for many characters, it is not always obvious which guideline to apply or in which order to apply several relevant guidelines. Different books about writing characters give different guidelines on stroke order, and the more advanced books have longer and more detailed lists of guidelines. In the following, look at the start of each group of characters for guidelines (if any) applicable to that group.

When lines intersect, you generally draw the horizontal line before the vertical.

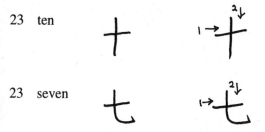

23   ten

23   seven

Characters that consist of a sequence of lines are written from top to bottom or from left to right.

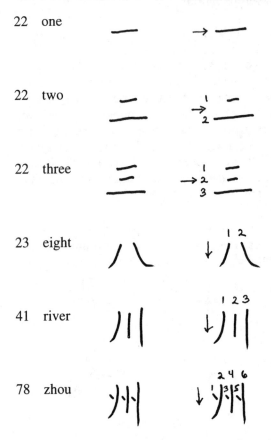

22 one

22 two

22 three

23 eight

41 river

78 zhou

Another way to write 州 is to first draw the three lines (same as 川 immediately above) from left to right and then fill in the three dots, also from left to right.

The following characters are also written from top to
bottom or from left to right.

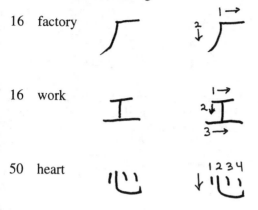

16 factory

16 work

50 heart

The following characters use a combination of the
top-to-bottom and horizontal-before-vertical guidelines mentioned earlier.

66 king

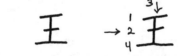

Overall, work from top to bottom: First draw
the — on top, then the + in the middle, then the
— on the bottom. The + is drawn like *ten* (horizontal before vertical, see page 113).

66 jade

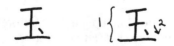

First draw 王 (as shown immediately above),
then add the dot.

The following characters use a combination of the top-to-bottom and left-to-right guidelines mentioned earlier.

56   public

Draw the top part (from left to right, same as *eight* 八 on page 114), then the bottom part (also from left to right).

41   cloud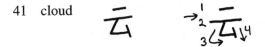

Draw the top part (from top to bottom, same as *two* 二 on page 114), then the bottom part (from left to right).

61   yuan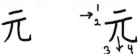

First draw the top part (the horizontal lines, top to bottom), then draw the bottom part (the legs, left to right).

22   six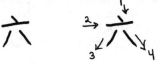

First draw the top part (top before bottom), then the bottom (left before right).

69   no

Draw the top line, then the bottom part from left to right.

37   down

37   up

52   north

Draw the left half before the right half.

22   five

14   school

First draw the top part, working from top to bottom and left to right. Then draw the bottom part, working from top to bottom.

The following characters use a combination of the left-to-right, horizontal-before-vertical, and top-to-bottom guidelines mentioned earlier.

19   enter

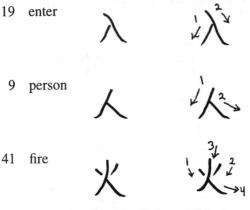

9   person

41   fire

Draw the dots first (left to right), then *person* 人 (shown immediately above).

14   big

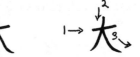

Draw the horizontal line first, then *person* 人 (shown above).

27   heaven

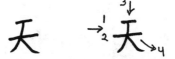

Think of 天 either as horizontal lines first (top to bottom), then the other lines (left to right, same as *person* 人 above); or as top (horizontal line) first, then bottom (the character 大 just shown).

20 close

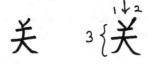

First draw the top dots (left to right), then draw the bottom part (same as the character 天 shown on the facing page).

20 open

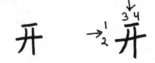

First draw the horizontal lines (top to bottom), then draw the vertical lines (left to right).

31 year

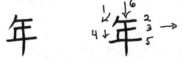

Working from top to bottom, draw the top part first (left before right), then the middle line, then the bottom part (top before bottom). Finally draw the vertical line.

Some miscellaneous characters:

41 mountain   山

Note that 山 is an exception to the usual left-to-right order.

20 exit   出

An empty box in any character is drawn like the character *mouth* 口.

19 mouth

23 product

Draw the boxes in the order shown (top to bottom, left to right). Each box is drawn like 口 (immediately above).

When there is stuff enclosed in a box, draw the box as for *mouth* 口 above, but draw the contents of the box before closing the box bottom.

27 sun

The inside of 日 is like *one* 一 (page 114).

11 field

The inside of 田 is like *ten* 十 (page 113).

66 nation

The inside of 国 is like *jade* 玉 (page 115).

---

57 park

園

The inside of 園 is like *yuan* 元 (page 116).

22 four

The inside of 四 is just left-to-right legs.

52 west

First draw the top line, then the box and the (left-to-right) legs. The legs are considered to be enclosed in the box, so draw them just before closing the box bottom.

In the following characters, the long vertical line that pierces the rest of the character is drawn last.

38 middle

中

中 is *mouth* 口 (facing page) with a line through it.

46 electric

電

电 is *sun* 日 (facing page) with a line through it.

A protruding middle stroke is drawn before symmetrical left and right parts.

14 small

42 water

The left and right sides of 水 are different, but it is symmetrical enough to follow this writing guideline.

42 tree

42 forest

Two *trees* (shown just above). When a character is made of side-by-side characters, draw the component characters from left to right.

69 prohibit

First draw the top part (the 林 character shown above), then the bottom part as shown here. The bottom is drawn top first (two lines, top to bottom), then bottom (protruding middle then left then right).

78   capital

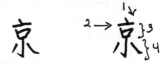

Working from top to bottom, draw the lid first
(top before bottom), then the box (see *mouth* 口
on page 120), and finally the bottom (same as
小 opposite).

Some miscellaneous characters:

48   vehicle

First draw the top part (horizontal before "vertical"), then the bottom part (with the strokes in
either order).

52   east

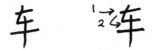

First draw the top part (horizontal before "vertical"), then the bottom part (protruding middle
then left then right, as for the characters in the
previous group).

When one part of a character shelters another part, draw the shelter first.

41 stone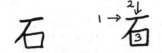

Draw the shelter first (top before bottom), then the box (see *mouth* 口, page 120).

38 right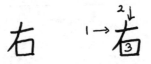

Draw the shelter first (horizontal before vertical), then the box (see *mouth* 口, page 120).

38 left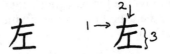

Draw the shelter first (horizontal before vertical), then *work* 工 (page 115).

16 store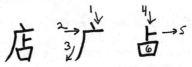

Draw the shelter first (top to bottom), then the inside part, again top to bottom. For the box, see *mouth* 口 (page 120).

71   can

可   司

Draw the shelter first (top before bottom), then
the box (see *mouth* 口, page 120). Another way
to write 可 is top (line) then left (box) then right
(line).

56   manage

司   司

Draw the shelter first, then the top (a line) before the bottom (a box, see *mouth* 口 on page
120).

Some miscellaneous characters:

23   nine

九   九

11   power

力

Draw the two strokes in either order. I think it
makes more sense to draw 力 like 九 (above).

Draw the outside (sheltering) part of a character before the inside (sheltered) part.

27 moon

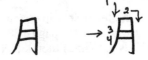

First draw the enclosure (from left to right), then the inside (from top to bottom).

56 use

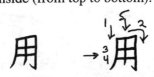

First draw the enclosure (same as that of 月, just above), then the inside (horizontal, from top to bottom, then vertical). Or draw a wide 月 (above) then add the center vertical line.

42 wind

52 south

First draw the top (same as *ten* 十, page 113), then the enclosure (same as for *moon* 月 and *use* 用 above), then the inside (top, from left to right; then bottom, horizontal before vertical).

68   city

市   　²→ 亠   　巾

First draw the top (top before bottom), then the enclosure (same as for *moon* 月 and *use* 用 opposite), then the inside line.

When a character consists of a combination of other characters, draw the component characters from left to right or from top to bottom. In addition to the characters shown below, this rule applies to *forest* 林 (page 122) and *product* 品 (page 120).

27   bright

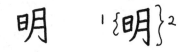

明　　¹{明}²

Sun 日 first (page 120), then *moon* 月 (page 126).

11   male

男　　男}¹₂

Field 田 first (page 120), then *power* 力 (page 125).

Some miscellaneous characters:

11   female

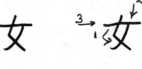

11   peace

First draw the roof, top to bottom and left to right, then put 女 (shown immediately above) under it.

20   gate

9   people

43   sea

First draw the "water radical" at the left, from top to bottom; note that the bottom line is drawn upward, which is unusual. Then draw the top, from left to right. Then draw the bottom part, putting the dots in last.

Pinyin and pronunciation

Pinyin uses the Latin alphabet with the addition of tone marks to indicate the pronunciation of Chinese syllables. It also uses apostrophes to separate syllables when necessary.

Tones

The pitch pattern, or *tone*, of a Chinese syllable is as much a part of the syllable as the vowel is. A *tone mark* is placed over the main vowel in each syllable to indicate one of four tones: steady high pitch, as in both syllables of *Xī'ān*; rising pitch, as in the *mén* of *Tiān'ānmén Square*; falling pitch, as in the first syllable of *Shànghǎi*; or falling then rising pitch, as in the second syllable of *Shànghǎi*. Although the tone is an integral part of the spoken syllable, the tone marks will often be omitted from Pinyin that you see in China (see the top figure on page 65).

Syllables and apostrophes

The apostrophes in *Xī'ān* and *Tiān'ānmén* are needed to separate syllables that might otherwise run together. *Xī'ān* without its apostrophe would look like one syllable instead of two, because *ia* is a legitimate vowel combination for the middle of a syllable. (Tone marks could indicate the number of syllables, but they are often omitted and are not used for this purpose.) *Tiān'ānmén* needs an apostrophe to show that the *n* between vowels is the end of one syllable, not the beginning of the next. (This kind of ambiguity rarely arises, because most consonants can only begin, never end, a syllable.)

Consonants

All consonants except **v** are used, as well as several combinations of consonants.

The following consonants, which may begin a syllable, are pronounced pretty much as in English:

b	**j**	**s**
ch	**k**	**sh**
d	**l**	**t**
f	**m**	**w** (but silent in
g (hard, as in	**n**	*wu*)
go)	**p**	**y** (but silent
h	**r**	before *u* or *i*)

The following consonants, which may end a syllable, are also pronounced pretty much as in English:

n	**ng**	**r**

The following consonants, which may begin a syllable, are pronounced pretty much like other English consonants:

c	like **ts**	**z**	like **dz**	**zh**	like **j**
q	like **ch**	**x**	like **sh**		

Some consonant sounds have two spellings (**ch** and **q** for the sound **ch**, **sh** and **x** for **sh**, **j** and **zh** for **j**) because some vowel pronunciations depend on the preceding consonant. For example, *shi* sounds like the beginning of *shirt*, but *xi* sounds like *she*.

Vowels

Vowel sounds depend on the combination of vowels and on what consonants (if any) start or end the syllable.

Here's what the basic vowels sound like:

a	<u>ah</u>, f<u>a</u>ther
e	teach<u>er</u>, French l<u>e</u>
but **ye = ie**	
i	mach<u>i</u>ne
i after **r,c,s,z,ch,sh,zh = e**	
o	<u>awe</u>, <u>o</u>ff
u	r<u>u</u>le
u after **j,q,x,y = ü**	
ü	German <u>ü</u>ber, French t<u>u</u>

Vowel combinations are pronounced as follows:

ai	<u>I</u>, <u>ai</u>sle	**ou**	<u>oh</u>, s<u>ou</u>l
ao	<u>ow</u>	**ua = wa**	
ei	<u>eigh</u>t	**uai = wai**	
ia = ya		**ui = wei**	
iao = yao		**uo = wo**	
ie	<u>ye</u>s	**üe = ü+e** as in **ie** above
iu = you			

The combinations ending with consonants are:

an	<u>an</u> or <u>on</u>	**in = i+n**	mach<u>ine</u>
but **yan = ian**		**ing**	s<u>ing</u>
ang = a+ng		**ong**	German
en	Ow<u>en</u>		j<u>ung</u>
eng	s<u>ung</u>	**uan = wan**	
er	<u>are</u> or h<u>er</u>	**uang = wang**	
ian	<u>yen</u>	**un = wen**	
iang = yang		**üan = üe+n**	
iong = yong		**ün = ü+n**	

Traditional characters

The table below shows the traditional forms of those characters in this book that are "simplified characters." The simplified character is followed here by its traditional form, the page number on which the character is explained, and the main English meaning.

学	學	14	school	风	風	42	wind
厂	廠	16	factory	电	電	46	electricity
门	門	20	gate	车	車	48	vehicle
开	開	20	open	东	東	52	east
关	關	20	close	园	園	57	park
云	雲	41	cloud	国	國	66	nation

You may wonder why in some cases, such as *gate*, an already-simple character was "simplified." This makes sense because some characters appear as parts of many other characters, so reducing the number of strokes in one such character reduces the number in many others.

Here are some hints on recognizing the most useful and common of these traditional forms. (Don't waste time on the others: *factory*, *close*, or *wind*.)

School: The two forms of *school* are the same on the bottom but different on top. Since *school* is often preceded by 大, 中, or 小 (Chapter 4), you will probably recognize this character in context.

Gate: The traditional form 門 is an easy-to-remember picture of a gate. *Gate* is a component of many other characters, and the simplified form of most of them was constructed by replacing the 門 with its simplified form 门. (*Open* and *close*, which are shown above, are exceptions to this rule.)

Open: The traditional form 開 is just the simplified form 开 inside a *gate* 門. *Open* is something you do to a *gate*.

Cloud, Electricity: The traditional form has the simplified form on the bottom and a chunk meaning *rain* on top. Clouds and electricity (lightning) are both associated with rain.

Vehicle, East: Think of 車 as a bird's-eye view of a two-wheeled cart: An axle (the vertical line) with a wheel near each end runs through the body of the cart. Think of 東 as a stretched-out *tree* 木 character with a *sun* 日 character inserted: *East* is where the rising sun is seen behind the trees. In both characters, the simplification involved replacing the 日 with an angled line and shortening the vertical line.

Park, Nation: Without learning the details inside the boxes, you can recognize these characters in certain contexts. For example, you know that *China* is *middle country*, so if you see 中 followed by a box with squiggly things in it, you will recognize the word as *China*. Similarly, if you're expecting to see the name of a park and you see 公 followed by a crowded box, you can recognize the word as *park*.

You can see the traditional characters for *gate*, *open*, and *nation* in the headlines on page 108, *cloud* in the figures on pages 69 and 77, and some others on page 134.

FIGURE 77: "Hong Kong University"

In Hong Kong (literally *fragrant harbor* — notice the water radical on the left side of *harbor*) the traditional character for *school* is used, as on this business card.

香港大學

FIGURE 78: "Pacific Bell Telephone Company"

Pacific Bell 電話公司

In California, Pacific Bell used traditional characters in its announcement of a new phone service. The two characters after *Bell* say *telephone* (*electric speech*). Compare this to the telephone signs on pages 47 and 57. The next word is explained on page 56.

FIGURE 79: "Vehicles" in Japan and Hong Kong

In Japan and Hong Kong, the traditional character for *vehicle* is used.

Right: *Rickshaw* ride for Japanese tourists visiting old Takayama. (If you can't read the rest of the sign, see page 86.)

Below: Victoria *Peak tram* (*mountain top cable vehicle*) in Hong Kong.

山頂纜車

FIGURE 80: "Peking Garden" restaurant, U.S.

In Massachusetts you'll see the traditional character for *park* or *garden*, as on this chopstick wrapper.

北京園

Explanations of figures

In some of the figures in this book, you were asked to understand some characters. Explanations of those figures are given here.

Figure 13: The bill was issued in 1979. The five characters are: *one, nine, seven, nine, year*.

Figure 14: The four years are as follows:

Beginning of paragraph: 1950 (*one, nine, five, O, year*).

Second line, after the period: 1951 (*one, nine, five, one, year*).

Third line, after the period: 1955 (*one, nine, five, five, year*).

Starting at end of fourth line and continuing on fifth line: 1980 (*one, nine, eight, O, year*).

I've written *O* instead of *zero* above because the big round O in the paragraph is the numeral *0* rather than the word *zero*.

Figure 15: The April calendar pages show the day of the week under the line that has *1988*, the lunar month on the bottom left (just under the lunar year), and the lunar date on the bottom right.
1988.4.23: Saturday (*week six*);
Third lunar month, eighth day.
1988.4.24: Sunday (*week sun*);
Third lunar month, ninth day.
The May calendar page shows the day of the week on the bottom left and the lunar date on the right.
1988.5.5: Thursday (*week four*)
Third lunar month, twentieth day.

Figure 16: The day of the week is right after the date (1988.4.25): It is *Monday* (*week one*). The lunar date is on the bottom line: It is the tenth day of the third month.

Figure 18: The three labels say: *above, below left,* and *below right.*

Figure 21: From right to left, we have *stone forest.* The Stone Forest is a dramatic area of eroded rock formations not far from Kunming.

Figure 41: Five people have surname *Wang* 王. The other characters taught in this book are 玉 (*jade*) and 国 (*nation*) from this chapter and 小 (*small*), 大 (*big*), 山 (*mountain*), 明 (*bright*), and 云 (*cloud*) from earlier chapters.

Figure 47: The first two characters under the Chinese for *Coca-Cola* say *China.* The fourth character on that line is *six.* The third and fourth characters on the next line say *Cola.*

Figure 51: The restaurant is in *Beihai Park* (first four characters after the colon).

Figure 52: The license plates are from *Yunnan* (top), *Beijing* (bottom left), and *Sichuan* (bottom right).

Figure 53: The right-hand tag is for *Beijing.*

Figure 54: The bottom destination is *Nanjing.*

Answers for Chapter 22

Puzzle 1

<u>Across</u>
1. mouth
2. middle school
3. caution!
4. university
6. exit

<u>Down</u>
2. center
3. elementary school
4. size
5. entrance

Puzzle 2

<u>Across</u>
1. product
2. 34
4. February
5. 50
6. sun, day of the month
7. January
8. moon, month

<u>Down</u>
2. March
3. April
4. 21

Puzzle 3

<u>Across</u>
1. field
2. 78
4. king
5. June
6. 90
7. year
8. city
9. May
10. peace

<u>Down</u>
2. July
3. August
5. 65

Puzzle 4

Across
1. November
2. December
4. 60
5. tomorrow
7. September
8. sky, heaven, day

Down
1. October
2. 16
3. 29
5. bright
6. daily

Puzzle 5

Across
1. everybody
3. public
4. The People's Park
7. manpower
8. woman

Down
1. everybody
2. the people
3. public park
5. company
6. man

Puzzle 6

Across
2. worker
4. population
5. factory
7. flint
9. volcano
10. masonry, mason
11. mountain pass

Down
1. grownup
3. artificial
6. jade
7. crater
8. carpentry, carpenter
9. volcano
10. Stone Forest

Puzzle 7

Across
1. middleman
2. thing
3. northwest
4. southeast
6. west gate
7. south wind

Down
1. Middle East
2. northeast
3. southwest
4. east gate
5. north wind

Puzzle 8

Across
1. 1948 (year)
3. river
5. 1956 (year)
8. October

Down
1. January 11(th)
2. Sichuan
4. school year
6. 50
7. June

Puzzle 9

Across
1. prohibit
2. below/lower right
3. above/upper left
4. (electric) switch
5. approximately
6. close (the door)
7. store
9. cannot
11. electric power
12. train

Down
2. below/lower left
3. above/upper right
4. open (the door)
8. water power
9. no, not
10. tasty
11. trolley
12. fire

Puzzle 10

Across
1. zhou (in place names)
3. yuan
4. Beihai Park
5. Nanjing person
7. Xi'an
8. Sun Yat-sen
9. sea
10. nation
11. Yunnan

Down
2. Shanghai person
4. Beijing
6. Tian'anmen
8. China
9. Hainan
11. cloud

Answers for Chapter 23

Figure 55: The left column says *caution* (small-heart), and the right column says *train* (fire-vehicle). The columns read from left to right, which is unusual — but just about any direction of writing may be seen on a short sign.

Figure 56: The first line says that *Chinese* (first two characters) *citizens* (next two characters) pay ¥0.20. The second line gives the price for *foreign tourists* (*foreign country tour people*, in which you may recognize the characters for *country* and *person*). The third line gives the price for *children* up to 1.2 meters tall (*1.2 meters under*). The character for *meter* also means *rice*; I assume it was chosen for *meter* because it is pronounced exactly like English *me*.

Figure 57: "Male use articles"

Figure 58: The sixth line gives the distance to the Stone Forest, which is 126 kilometers. You can tell that the distances are in metric units, since each number is followed by 公 (public). The other place names with characters taught in this book are:

Line 1: Dali, starting with *big* (*dà*)
Line 3: Zhongdian, starting with *middle* (*zhōng*)
Line 9: Baoshan, ending with *mountain* (*shān*)
Line 11: Tonghai, ending with *sea* (*hǎi*)
Line 12: Yuanmou, starting with *yuan* (which has meanings other than the denomination of money we learned about)

All these places are in Yunnan province.

Figure 59: To fill in a date, you would put numbers before the characters for *year*, *month*, and *day* on the bottom line. The receipt was issued by a Beijing factory (top line). The thing I bought goes in the second column, under the word *article* (*product*).

Figure 60: The first two characters say *jade*, and the last character means *factory*. The whole thing says "jade carving factory."

Figure 61: 20 kilograms.

In the middle of the picture you can find the character sequence *two ten public*. *Two ten* means 20, and *public* indicates that the unit is metric, so you can guess that the word must be *kilograms*.

Did you notice that there two kinds of comma in this figure? The funny-looking comma is used in a sequence of things, where we might say *and* or *or* in English. It also appears in Figure 45 (page 70) and Figure 70 (page 108).

Figure 62: The two-character words are:

(top) Northwest Industrial University (officially translated as Northwestern Polytechnical University); (bottom) China Xi'an. The country always precedes the city in Chinese.

Figure 63: Reading from right to left, the seven characters you can recognize say "Beijing…water company…under…fire…"

You can tell that it goes from right to left if you recognize either of the two-character words *Beijing* or *company*. The whole thing says "Beijing (characters 1-2) tap water (characters 3-5) company (characters 6-7) underground (characters 8-9, literally *ground under*) hydrant (characters 10-12)."

Figure 64: The first three characters reading down say *Mao Zedong*. Near the end of the column you should find *ninety*, then (after an unfamiliar character) the word *year*.

Figure 65: The first line reads "1974 March." The next line starts with "west peace," which is Xi'an, and two characters later we see *east*, so the find was east of Xi'an. Near the end of that line is *mountain* (or *hill*), and soon after it *under*; the find was at the foot of a hill.

Figure 66: Note that the writing goes from top to bottom, and the things that look like colons are colons. The cable number is on the left — 1355. Then comes the phone number — 53966. The address starts with *Xi'an municipality*; the characters *small* and *east* are part of the street name; and *three* is the street address. (The character after *east* means *road* — same as in Figure 1 on page 10 and Figure 50 on page 80. The character after *three* means *number* — you can also find it in the figures on page 81.) Addresses are always written with the largest unit (in this case the city) first.

Figure 67: Here are the parts you might recognize:

The vehicle is described in the first line (first character *small*, last character *vehicle*).

Two people (end of the bottom line) *can/may* (first character on bottom line) ride at once.

The price is *one yuan* (end of third line).

The only other number in the sign is *three* (second line), which is the number of times you can go around the track for that price.

Figure 68: The top line says "Beijing municipal trolley company"

Figure 69: The first two characters say *Beijing*. From the fourth character (*under*) and the seventh (*vehicle*) you can guess that this is a subway ticket. The whole line says "Beijing subway vehicle ticket." *Subway* is a four-character word in which the first two characters mean *underground* (literally *ground under*).

Also, by comparing the big characters in the second line to the figures in Chapter 17, you can figure out that the ticket cost *two jiao*.

Figure 70: Shanghai, April 24; Xi'an, April 24; Beijing, April 22.

By the way, this newspaper, being intended for overseas distribution, uses traditional characters rather than simplified characters. The bottom headline starts with *China*, using the traditional character for *nation*. The middle headline contains *gate* (second character) and *open* (sixth character).

Figure 71: The bottom line means *do not enter*, which you can tell from the second character (*prohibit*) and the third (*enter*). Literally, the four characters are *strictly prohibited enter inside*. The top line says *protect lawn*.

Were you confused by the *enter* character because there's a gap between the two lines? The fact that the right stroke clearly sticks out past the left makes this an understandable *enter* (as opposed to *eight*). Even Chinese people can get this confused: A friend of mine took a picture of an entrance sign in China that clearly said *eight mouth* instead of *enter mouth* (the separate strokes did not overlap).

Figure 72: "Beijing battery factory"

Beijing – 1st and 2nd characters;

battery – 3rd and 4th characters, literally *electric pool* (notice the water radical on the left of *pool*);

factory – last character.

The two big characters at the top also say *Beijing*.

Figure 73: You could recognize the first, second, and fourth characters. The first two characters are *mountain on*, which means *on the mountain* (as explained on page 39). The fourth character tells you the sign prohibits something. It is plausible that the thing prohibited is smoking, because the left half of the last character is the character for *fire*. (A character within a character sometimes hints at the meaning of the whole character.)

Literally, the whole sign says *mountain on strictly forbidden smoke* (each of these English words corresponding to one character, except for *smoke*, which corresponds to the last two characters). Compare this sign to the bottom figure on page 70: The last four characters of this sign are the same as the first four in that figure.

Figure 74: The sign says "Only dissolves your mouth, not dissolves your hand." You may recognize *mouth* and *not*, which together with the separation of the two parts of the slogan makes it plausible that the slogan is as expected. Also, though you don't know the word *dissolve*, you can recognize the water radical on its left side, which makes it plausible that it has to do with melting. The left piece of the word *your/you* is called the *person radical*. It is a distortion of the character 人 (*person*), and appears on the left side of many characters whose meaning has to do with people.

Figure 75: The first two characters say *Nanjing*, the next two mean *Sun Yat-sen* (literally, *middle mountain*), and the fifth is *mausoleum*. The two-character phrase is *mausoleum gate*. You could recognize all of these characters but *mausoleum*. Since the Chinese you recognize is *Nanjing Sun Yat-sen* [?] followed by [?] *gate*, and the two unknown characters are the same, it would be a good guess that the unknown character means *mausoleum*.

Figure 76: We can guess that the first two characters in the title mean *Tibet*, because they appear twice in the title, once preceding the word *person*, and we know that a *Tibetan* in Chinese would be a *Tibet person* (see page 79). Notice that *Tibet* starts with *west*, which makes sense geographically.

The next line starts with *China* and contains *exit* twice, each time followed by the same character. *Exit* also means to issue, in the sense of publishing, so this repeated two-character word probably corresponds to *published* and *press* in the English. (Actually, there's a three-character word *publishing house* followed by a two-character word *publish*.) This line does not, however, have *Beijing, China* in it. The single occurrence of *China* apparently belongs to the name of the publisher.

Recommended books

The China Guidebook, by Fredric M. Kaplan, Julian M. Sobin, and Arne J. de Keijzer, is unusual in that it gives the name of each city — as well as the names of all attractions, hotels, and restaurants — in Chinese characters. This is also a superb guidebook.

Fun with Chinese Characters, by Tan Huay Peng, is a delightful, lighthearted introduction to characters. The three volumes give the origin and stroke order of 469 characters, along with cartoons and other mnemonic aids. Most of the simpler characters are in the first volume. Simplified characters are taught, but the traditional forms are also shown.

Reading and Writing Chinese, by William McNaughton, is excellent if you want to embark on a more thorough study of Chinese characters. It is most useful if you are learning the language too, but is still usable if you are not. Traditional characters are taught, but the simplified forms are also shown.

The Chinese Language: Fact and Fantasy, by John DeFrancis, is the book to read if you want to know more about the relationship of the spoken language and its written forms, whether or not you know any spoken or written Chinese. This is a serious book, but not at all dry. The author conveys a wealth of trustworthy information in a very readable manner, largely by describing and debunking the many popular myths about Chinese.

The Pinyin Chinese-English Dictionary is a full-scale dictionary in which the Chinese characters (and compound words that start with those characters) are arranged alphabetically by their pronunciation — that is, by their Pinyin spelling. You can look up any character whose Pinyin spelling you know, and get a detailed definition along with examples of usage and multi-character words or phrases that start with that character. There are also some smaller dictionaries based on this one.

Subject Index

Pinyin Index

With this index, you can find the characters for a name or a one-syllable word from its Pinyin spelling. If a figure number is given, the corresponding word is illustrated in that figure but is not taught in the text.

You can try to guess the characters for a multi-syllable Pinyin word that is not shown here as follows. Let's say you are going to stay at the Dongfeng Hotel in Chengdu. You find entries for *dong* and *feng* below, which lead you to the characters for *east* and *wind*. Your hotel is, in fact, named *East Wind*. (Of course, you might not get the right answer, since there are many other characters spelled *dong* and *feng* that are not in this book.)

English Word Index

This index tells you where the characters for the given English words are taught. A figure number means that the word is illustrated in that figure but not taught in the text.

Quick Reference

Here are all the characters taught in this book — each followed by the page on which it is taught and by its main English meaning. To look up a character by its meaning, use the English Word Index.

人 人	9	person	出	20	exit
民	9	people	门	20	gate
女	11	female	开	20	open
男	11	male	关	20	close
力	11	power	一	22	one
田	11	field	二	22	two
安	11	peace	三	22	three
大	14	big	四 四	22	four
小	14	small	五	22	five
学	14	school	六	22	six
工	16	work	七	23	seven
厂	16	factory	八 八	23	eight
品	16	product	九	23	nine
店	16	store	十	23	ten
口	19	mouth	日	27	sun
入 入	19	enter	月	27	moon

天	27	heaven
明	27	bright
年	31	year
上	37	up
下	37	down
中	38	middle
左	38	left
右	38	right
山	41	mountain
川	41	river
火	41	fire
云	41	cloud
石	41	stone
风	42	wind
木	42	tree
林	42	forest
水	42	water
海	43	sea
电	46	electric
车	48	vehicle

心	50	heart
东	52	east
南	52	south
西	52	west
北	52	north
公	56	public
司	56	manage
用	56	use
园	57	park
元	61	yuan
国	66	nation
玉	66	jade
王	66	king
市	68	city
不	69	no
禁	69	prohibit
可	71	can
京	78	capital
州	78	zhou